THE LIBRARY MAN OF INDIA

THE LIBRARY MAN OF INDIA

THE STORY OF **P.N. Panicker**

P.P. SATHYAN

with inputs from

N. BALAGOPAL AND RAJEEV NAIR

RUPA

Published by
Rupa Publications India Pvt. Ltd 2024
7/16, Ansari Road, Daryaganj
New Delhi 110002

Sales centres:
Bengaluru Chennai
Hyderabad Jaipur Kathmandu
Kolkata Mumbai Prayagraj

P-ISBN: 978-93-5702-399-3
E-ISBN: 978-93-5702-168-5

First impression 2024

10 9 8 7 6 5 4 3 2 1

Printed in India

CONTENTS

FOREWORD

The life and times of the late P.N. Panicker need to be told and retold. This dreamer, with extraordinary tenacity and resilience, was the architect of the library revolution that catalysed the emergence of a modern Kerala. Today, Kerala is being hailed as the first state that has attained universal literacy. In school enrolment, girls' education and other indices, Kerala has a trailblazing history. In social development parameters, this small state has sometimes, with fair justification, been compared to developed countries of Western Europe. All these accomplishments have been possible because of widespread awareness and acceptance of the value of the written word and the importance of reading.

Great religious and social reformers like Narayana Guru had always emphasized that the liberating value of education alone could trigger sustainable social changes. However, while rightly focussing attention on expanding formal school education and making it accessible to all, the need to educate the older generations and society at large and expose them to the enriching delight of reading got sidelined. It was P.N. Panicker's lifelong mission to establish libraries even in the remotest villages of the state that provided the fertile ground for modernity to flower. All educational attainments of the state could be sustained and anchored only because of the growth of literacy among the rural people and their engagement with the written word. The contribution of the library movement in shaping the egalitarian, political and social vision should not be overlooked.

I had the good fortune of having P.N. Panicker as my acquaintance in my younger days as a rural library functionary and later as the district collector of Kozhikode. He was always full of energy; nothing could discourage him and no reverses or obstacles could dissuade him. Such was the intensity of his vision and the courage of conviction that light would eventually shine on his chosen path. He had the patience and faith to wait and the willingness to sacrifice personal comforts. Ordinary obstacles would naturally melt away in front of a person with such enormous willpower and inspiration. He travelled the length and breadth of the state several times, spreading the simple but potent message: 'Read and Grow'. With his handholding and inspiration, hundreds of libraries were established in the towns and villages of Kerala. Young and old discovered the joys and value of reading. Progressive ideas percolated into the minds of the people through these libraries. The ideals of an egalitarian society based on human dignity and equality were getting translated into reality.

Panicker had started his engagement with libraries in the mid-1940s. The Grandhasala Sangham that he set up became a pioneering institution that has been taken over by the government today as an apex body of a few thousand libraries in the state. It would be a travesty of truth if we assume that Panicker's accomplishments were easy and painless. This book throws light on the lesser-known facts of his life and the several sacrifices his family had to make. A true Gandhian throughout his life, Panicker was an epitome of righteousness and rectitude in public life. As moral benchmarks of public life are constantly being compromised, the life of P.N. Panicker shines as a blazing beacon on a darkening shore.

In the first century of the new millennium, humanity has witnessed unprecedented technological changes that directly impact our lives. The changes are poised to acquire greater strength and momentum, with refinements in artificial intelligence, machine learning and other emerging technologies. The common theme that underlies these changes of gargantuan proportions is the primacy of knowledge and the multiplier effect of networking. As the world is experiencing the creative turbulence of a knowledge economy that slowly elbows out ideas and attitudes at odds with these new priorities, it is only befitting that we recall the contribution of a man of frail frame who laid rock-solid foundations of knowledge architecture in Kerala more than seven decades ago. Such far-sightedness is indeed rare. Even rarer is that benevolent tenacity.

This crisp volume has done justice to an eventful life by contextualizing Panicker's life and struggle in the sociopolitical history of Kerala. I fervently wish that the millennial generation reads this book. The life and work of P.N. Panicker would familiarize them with the true power of dreams and the zest that can realize them. This book speaks at once to several generations. For the not-so-young readers, it brings to life a bygone era of idealism and probity in public life. For the young, it would provide a moral compass to negotiate a purposeful life amidst reverses, temptations, turbulence and frustrations.

—K. Jayakumar
Former Chief Secretary of Kerala;
Founding Vice-Chancellor of Thunchath Ezhuthachan
Malayalam University;
Poet, Translator and Author

1

A LITERARY GIANT

Among the luminaries of modern Kerala, P.N. Panicker occupies a significant space. We owe gratitude to the great lover of letters and books for his unforgettable sacrifice of waging a cultural crusade against illiteracy in Kerala. He was a legendary hero who valiantly fought to eradicate illiteracy, bringing about mass education in Kerala. He was a strong advocate of freedom and democratic practices, exemplifying his profound commitment to these ideals throughout his life. P.N. Panicker was an extraordinary individual who imbibed simplicity, sincerity, humility and virtuousness. Politically and culturally, he was inspired by Mahatma Gandhi but never chose the life of a politician. Gandhi was the personification of Karma Yoga theory which states that the ultimate goal of human life is to fulfil karma regardless of its after-effects. The 'Karma theory' (theory of work) and 'Jnana theory' (theory of wisdom) are twin ideas of Indian philosophy that Gandhi stressed.

The dawn of the twentieth century was a brilliant era in the history of India, and Kerala specifically, as it marked the change from the pre-modern era to the modern era, characterized by national and cultural awakenings. This period witnessed a strong resurgence in the fields of politics and culture. P.N. Panicker is widely acclaimed as the 'Rajarshi of Library' (the term 'Rajarshi' comes from Sanskrit and denotes a king who possesses deep knowledge—philosopher king) and the father of the cultural renaissance in Kerala. It was also the time of great personalities like Mahatma Gandhi, Rabindranath Tagore and Narayana Guru.

The renaissance movement in Kerala led by Narayana Guru, Vaikunda Swami, Ayyankali, Thycaud Ayya, Guru Chattampi Swamikal, Brahmananda Swami Sivayogi, Dr Palpu, C. Krishnan, Kumaran Asan, Vakkom Moulavi, Pandit Karuppan, T.K. Madhavan, Poykayil Appachan and others had ushered in a new era. This movement put an end to the dark age of feudalism and sowed the seeds of ideas like freedom of thought, freedom of expression, religious freedom, political freedom, gender equality, human rights, universal suffrage, individual freedom, socialism, etc. Without a cultural renaissance, politics would have no roots, and without a political mission, renaissance bears no fruit: both are reciprocal and redemptive. As the father of cultural renaissance in Kerala, P.N. Panicker strove relentlessly to shape a society based on a new political conscience, cultural consciousness, universal literacy, mass education, computer literacy and social safety.

Since time immemorial, Kerala has been the land of miracles and magic for foreigners with its vast and varied resources enchanting travellers. Though Kerala is abundant in many precious materials, the greatest resource of the land is its cultural heritage ingrained in the outlook of the new generation. This cultural heritage is nothing but the exalted ideals of religious harmony, love for freedom and love for wisdom.

DIVERSITY

The culture of Kerala has long been fascinating and diverse, arousing the enthusiasm of scintillating geniuses across various realms of life. Kerala's culture acquired momentum during the first half of the twentieth century. This radiant era was characterized by the flourishing of poetry, paintings, novels and more. Kumaran Asan and Vallathol Narayana Menon were prominent Malayalam poets who motivated readers with their unparalleled and exceptional genius. While Vallathol was highly inspired by nationalistic ideas, Kumaran Asan was smitten by the spiritual halo of Narayana Guru who instilled in his disciple's mind the principles of annihilation of caste and untouchability. The caste system was the most inhuman thing that humankind witnessed. For more than a thousand years, Indian society has been in the grip of casteism and untouchability. In ancient times, Buddha, Mahavira, Basaveshwara and other reformers staunchly fought against the severity of casteism and untouchability, tirelessly striving to emancipate society from their stranglehold.

The clarion call for renaissance was sounded by reformers like Raja Ram Mohan Roy, Swami Vivekananda, Narayana Guru and E.V. Ramasamy 'Periyar', heralding a revolutionary era in the history of India. The marvellous offshoots of the dazzling epoch were the colourful growth of literary, cultural and artistic creations that enriched the country. The origin and growth of the press resulted in the popularization of media and literary creations with many celebrated journalists appearing in the cultural arena of Kerala. The newspapers played an important role in awakening the political conscience of the people. In the realm of novels, O. Chandu Menon was the first writer who contributed a major novel called *Indulekha,* which highlighted issues related to the right to freedom, gender equality and right to education. Kumaran Asan's *Chinthavishtayaya Seetha* deconstructed masculine hegemony deeply rooted in Indian society. In all the major works of Asan, readers will feel the robust ideals of the equality of women, emancipation of women and annihilation of caste.

Vallathol, who has been acclaimed as the national poet of Kerala, wrote poems like *Kochu Seetha,* which breathed new life into the culture of Kerala. Malayalam literature blossomed to give expression to the creativity of life that had been suppressed for many years.

It was in this cultural and political context that the great cultural and social activist P.N. Panicker rose to prominence in the social arena of Kerala. From his humble beginning, he shot to fame, astonishing many armchair intellectuals, bureaucratic academicians and sycophantic political leaders. Hailing from a middle-class peasant family, Panicker was a primary school teacher by profession.

The society in which we live is patriarchal, unconditionally patronizing people who are immensely rich and highly influential in society. In the arena of politics, art and education, mediocre people attain stardom as they possess either a royal ancestral name or considerable wealth. Panicker was devoid of those possessions. As Gandhiji and Narayana Guru gained prominence, Panicker—a short and thin man with his unusual industriousness, humility, perseverance, punctiliousness, deep insight, far-sightedness, truthfulness and, above all, love for egalitarianism and wisdom—rose to the noblest level of our cultural history. His era marked a blissful period of cultural enlightenment and the blossoming of inspiring connoisseurs from all walks of life.

The saga of P.N. Panicker's life should be made into a textbook for students so that posterity can learn the lessons of a selfless and honest life to make their lives worthy. Panicker's life itself is a textbook, a living and unique book with a pulsating heart. Beyond his love for his children, he loved his self-selected career. Panicker's career, as Karl Marx wrote while he was a college student, 'was the career of a social worker', or more technically, a social activist; or as Bernard Shaw wrote, 'My profession is my hobby and my hobby is my profession'; or as Gandhi's cherished philosophy put in his own words, 'My message is my life'.

The social and cultural awakening of Kerala was enriched by numerous movements and organizations that were the hallmark of the enlightened period. Gandhi assimilated Rabindranath Tagore's quintessential concept of 'Shantiniketan', formulating a novel pedagogy and epistemology of education that was hailed as the 'Basic Educational Policy'. Panicker had a dream, a dream that was cherished by Gandhi, Narayana Guru and Booker T. Washington. From a dystopic world filled with fallacy and mirages, he became the cultural father of Kerala. The crowning beauty of his sacrificial life was the resurrection of a society that had surrendered to age-old customs and rituals. Gandhi's emphasis on village life in India had a deep and far-reaching impact on political and social history. Western concepts of material development were sharply problematized through the potential norms of the so-called 'Asiatic Society'. Gandhi put forward the new concept of 'Gram Swaraj', essentially discarding the

Western concept of a totalitarian state. His ideals of democracy were moulded by the indigenous concepts of self-sufficient villages and natural ways of living.

There were several leaders in Kerala who were inspired by Gandhi. The first name to be mentioned is barrister G.P. Pillai, the only person from Kerala mentioned in Gandhiji's autobiography, *My Experiments with Truth*. K. Kelappan, widely known as 'Kerala Gandhi', Mohammed Abdur Rahiman Sahib and M.P. Manmadhan were also followers of Gandhiji. P. Krishna Pillai, who became the leader of the communist party of Kerala, was initially inspired by Gandhiji. He took part in the Salt Satyagraha and was also a staunch member of the Temple Entry Movement in Kerala. A.K. Gopalan was also initially inspired by Gandhiji and later became the national leader of the Communist Party of India. P.N. Panicker, born and brought up amidst various political experiments, grew up in the cradle shaped by his foremost contemporaries.

Gandhi had a bitter political experience while he was in South Africa. Though he assimilated invaluable lessons from there, it was from the history of India that he absorbed the fundamental lessons in politics. It was nothing but the question of caste, entirely different yet fundamentally similar to the apartheid policy of South Africa. By grappling with the question of caste, Gandhi realized a great truth—if the task of eliminating casteism and uplifting the downtrodden classes failed, India's freedom would be futile. That was why he became the political ambassador of the Temple Entry Movement initiated by the Hindu Mahasabha in India.

Ever since Hindu society was divided into four varnas and numerous castes, it was the prerogative of the Brahmins to perform all rites related to temples. Being the upper-caste, they usurped many community temples and brahmanized them. Casteism was deep-rooted in the society of Kerala. Even Narayana Guru had no right to walk along public roads. When Gandhi came to Kerala to launch 'Ayithochadanam' (elimination of untouchability), he was forbidden to enter the house of an upper-caste Hindu; in order to receive Gandhiji, the house owner built a shelter outside the house. The downtrodden classes could walk only under the cover of forests and bushes. It was such a dehumanizing time that the Dalits in Kerala convened a conference known as 'Kayal Sammelanam' in the backwaters of the Cochin Lake.

With the introduction of the English language and the consequent spread of knowledge, many progressive ideas began to change the mindset of people from Kerala. Several educated youth hailing from different castes, classes and religions became increasingly conscious of the imperatives of changing society. Thus, along with the luminaries already mentioned earlier, reformers like Mannathu Padmanabhan, E.M.S. Namboodiripad, M.P. Bhattathiripad and others also played an active role in changing the social scenario of Kerala. It is, however, not possible here to elucidate the examples of all renaissance currents in Kerala. Renaissance was not a unipolar movement like nationalism. It is in a strictly cognitive context that we make out a distinctive cultural map for P.N. Panicker.

He was an able organizer. However, in the age of globalization, the internet and computers, the term 'organizer' has become obsolete and been replaced by 'event manager'. The most hilarious aspect apropos of Panicker is that he was very prognostic in the popularization of cyberspace. Formally speaking, Panicker was neither a scholar nor a bookworm. But more than any other scholar or academician, he loved reading and was a pioneer of popularizing reading among the people of Kerala. He inspired children, women and even the elderly to not only read and write but also to use computers and the internet.

It is indescribable to convey how Panicker, in a society where transport and communication were not as developed as today, travelled the entire length and breadth of Kerala using only his legs as his vehicle. He may be the first cultural leader in India to cover such long distances on foot. He was not only an activist who inspired millions of people to read and write but also an unparalleled cultural leader who instilled in people the necessity of living a life full of noble ideas. He taught people the importance of reading books to bring about social change. His mission was to transform the old society into a vibrant, modern one. He aimed for total literacy of the people, urging them to discard dehumanizing systems of dowry, untouchability, subservience of women, superstitions, religious intolerance, casteism and child marriage.

Being the foremost proponent of the library and literacy movements in Kerala, Panicker should be acclaimed and hailed as the founder or father of the cultural renaissance of Kerala. It was Narayana Guru who, as the founder of social renaissance, laid the groundwork for social justice and social equality to prevail. The renaissance in Kerala diverged significantly from the model of the Bengal Renaissance—if the Bengal Renaissance was characterized as a movement of the upper or elite class, the renaissance of Kerala was a subaltern movement. In other words, the Kerala Renaissance was an alternative modernism shaped by subaltern thinkers and leaders who envisioned a parallel world where all men and women would be able to live as equals. Narayana Guru advocated the divine ideals of 'one caste, one religion, one God for humanity', emphasizing the goodness of all individuals irrespective of their religious beliefs.

Panicker, the unparalleled stalwart of the people's library movement in Kerala, championed the cause of universal reading and writing. To achieve this goal, he put aside all worldly pleasures and leisure. Leading a life of wanderlust, he was passionate about letters and books. As the chief architect of the modern library movement, he interacted with people from all walks of life and demonstrated compassion towards his co-workers and the people. The annual remembrance day of P.N. Panicker on 19 June is observed as the 'Day of Reading' by the Kerala government. Coinciding with this, Prime Minister Narendra Modi issued a call in 2017 to celebrate the period from 19 June to 18 July as the 'Reading Month' across the entire country.

When Prime Minister Modi inaugurated the 22nd National Reading Day held at Kochi, he stated the following:

> P.N. Panicker left an indelible mark at the national level. The National Literacy Mission has been inspired largely by his work.
>
> I commend the government of Kerala for setting up an institution to perpetuate the memory of P.N. Panicker. I am very happy that the P.N. Panicker Vigyan Vikas Kendra is taking the lead to make Kerala the first e-literate state of the country in collaboration with the central and state governments and civil society organizations.
>
> The total e-literacy campaign to be implemented using the tools of Information and Communication Technology (ICT) will help in reducing the digital

> divide. This will contribute to improvements in the living standards of the underprivileged population of the state.
>
> I am told that the P.N. Panicker Foundation, the mother organization of the P.N. Panicker Vigyan Vikas Kendra, was the first organization in the country to popularize e-reading among the rural masses. I am happy that the Vigyan Vikas Kendra is taking this work forward.

On the eve of the closing ceremony of the centenary birthday celebrations of P.N. Panicker held at Thiruvananthapuram on 13 August 2010, former President of India Pratibha Devisingh Patil delivered the inaugural speech. In her address, she fondly remembered P.N. Panicker, stating, 'His vision, his identification with the common people and his commitment to improve their lives has made him a legendary figure, worth emulating.'

Patil further stated:

> Considered one of the principal architects of modern Kerala, P.N. Panicker lived a life to the cause of libraries and the development of the state. Panicker was deeply interested in educating agricultural workers and encouraging them to study, and its relevance persists even today. His area of work gradually expanded. With his 'Read and Grow' slogan, the library and literacy movements started by him spread

to every nook and corner of Kerala. So impactful was his work through the Akshara Keralam Project that Kerala became the first fully literate state in the country in 1991. [...]

The government of Kerala, every year observes June 19, the day Panicker passed away, as the Vayanadinam, the Day of Reading. Inculcating the habit of reading in children and youth is very important. Besides being a source of knowledge, reading develops their mental ability and improves concentration levels. This is especially important in our times, as children have many other sources of entertainment which provide instant gratification, such as television, the internet, electronic games and social networking sites. The challenge is to make our children read more and attract them to read books that tell them about our heritage and cultural values. [...] Panicker was also a man who was a firm believer in Gandhiji's concept of living a simple life, usually clad in Khadi, a frail figure, he was warmly welcomed wherever he travelled in Kerala. Individuals like Panicker have taught us that a life of values, commitment to a cause and selfless service can bring many positive changes in society.

Before the modern library missions initiated by Panicker, libraries did exist in Kerala. However, the most praiseworthy initiative undertaken by the great organizer was the establishment of the people's library and literacy movements in Kerala. Under his leadership, thousands of reading centres (grandhalayams) were built across the state. By popularizing reading and writing, P.N. Panicker revolutionized the realm of the library (which was the monopoly of the elite class) by democratizing it to the grassroots level.

2

EARLY LIFE

Puthuvayil Narayana Panicker, fondly called 'Nanu', was born on 1 March 1909 in Neelamperoor village, Kottayam district. Puthuvayil was the ancestral home, the home of his mother, Janakippillai. Govinda Pillai, his father, hailed from a Brahmin family and had a strict spiritual orientation. The Puthuvayil family was a joint family under the matriarchal system where children lived in the home of their mother. Nanu had an elder brother, Kesava.

Nanu, a curious boy, received a rudimentary education from Ittanasan, a teacher in the village school called Nattu Pallikoodam. The school was situated one and a half miles from Neelamperoor. Nanu travelled to school by passing through the emerald rice fields, rejoicing in the captivating sight of ponds and lakes that flooded in the rainy season.

Neelamperoor village has gained prominence through the festival Pooram Padayani, drawing fascination and attendance from both locals and outsiders. The village is now very popular after it came to be known as the birthplace of figures like P.N. Panicker, Neelamperoor Madhusoodanan Nair and several renowned Kathakali artists. It is now a part of Alappuzha district, which was formed in 1957.

From childhood, Nanu exhibited a habit of reading books and was not only a voracious reader but also a judicious one too, making notes from the texts. He also had a well-stocked library in his home. Following Buddha, the great philosopher who urged people to abandon desire, Nanu also found liberation. However, the one desire that remained was his desire to read and promote reading.

Nanu was brought up in an atmosphere of piety and spirituality. The Puthuvayil house is situated in close proximity to the Neelamperoor Palli Bhagavathi Temple. Regular visits to the temple, accompanied by prayers and hymns, created a spiritual atmosphere at home. Recitation of the *Ramayana* and the *Bhagavad Gita* was part of Nanu's spiritual orientation. His father instilled the essence of Hinduism's salvation theory—the theory of 'moksha'. Along with these he also assimilated the aesthetic charm of the epics, the *Ramayana* and the *Mahabharata*. The result of this was that Nanu became a staunch follower of dharma, truth and sacrifice, upholding the foundational teachings of Hinduism centred on righteousness and justice.

After the completion of primary education, Nanu studied at Vazhappilly and Kurichi, then he joined

Changanassery High School, where he passed the Elementary School Leaving Certificate (ESLC) exam with flying colours. Unfortunately, the family's financial difficulties became an obstacle to his higher studies. His father died when he was studying in the fifth standard and the responsibility of looking after the family fell upon Kesavan, Nanu's elder brother, who fulfilled it benignly. To shoulder the responsibility of caring for his family, Nanu accepted a career as a schoolteacher at the Neelamperoor Middle School. Panicker was later transferred from Neelamperoor to Ambalappuzha where he took charge of the primary school. In his teaching career, he also worked as a teacher in Vakathanam, Vazhappally, Kurumpanadom, Pala and Kidangoor schools.

As a teacher, Panicker was a role model. Teachers play a vital role in the intellectual and ethical development of students. He believed that teaching was more than an intellectual exercise—it was an art form—a righteous and delicate way of moulding the character and temperament of the pupils. Teachers, in his view, are the embodiment of egalitarian values, acting as engineers of the spirit of students. Nanu was the personification of the ideal teacher who aroused a solemn inspiration and orientation in the hearts of the students. His deep affection, ethical instructions, benevolent treatment, strict discipline, insistence on righteousness and reasoning cultivated a new culture in the hearts and minds of the students. Nanu master encouraged—rather stimulated—students to read books, echoing Shakespeare's sentiment that, 'A beggar's book outworths a noble's blood.' Throughout his life, Nanu strived to live up to the meaning of these words, dedicating himself to fight a Herculean battle to eradicate illiteracy and ignorance. His watchwords, 'read and grow' and 'think and be wise' reverberated melodiously across the country. Even today, the whole nation is striving to hold the torch lit by him.

While he was working as a teacher, Panicker studied for the Malayalam Vidvan Pareeksha. He also studied Hindi, inspired by Gandhiji. Thus, Panicker embraced the dual role of a teacher and a student. As a man of progressive ideas, Panicker had sworn to abstain from superstitions and religious and social practices. In this respect, his convictions were shaped by the confluence of two influential movements of his time: the national movement led by Gandhiji and the social renaissance movement heralded by Narayana Guru.

Panicker fought against the social and cultural discrimination that had prevailed in Kerala for ages. He also addressed economic inequalities that hindered the overall progress of society. His life was virtually a challenge against a caste-ridden and class-hegemonized social system. He actively participated in getting rid of the age-old social practice of dowry and championed the cause of the destitute, the segregated, the abandoned, the suppressed, the tortured and the exploited. Panicker's personal life served as a paradigm for politicians and social activists. He eliminated the imaginary wall put up between the private and public lives of individuals—Panicker repudiated it as a social myth and discarded it from his life. This was one of the reasons why he was respected, loved and adored by the people regardless of their social and economic status. Panicker strove to achieve the set goals of his life: uplifting the downtrodden through reading, writing and thinking. His fight for universal education through the Kerala Association for Non-Formal Education (KANFED) marked a transformative shift in Kerala's social landscape. His mantra 'Read and Grow' invigorated society as a whole. Inspired by Gandhi's endeavour to launch 'Harijanodhaaranam', Panicker tirelessly worked towards a similar mission for adult literacy in Kerala.

3

THE 'PADAYANI' OF LIBRARY

The word theophany originates from 'theo', meaning God, and 'phany', meaning appearance or manifestation. It is a fusion of Latin and Greek, denoting the belief that God appears on solemn occasions at the sanctum sanctorum (usually at shrines). The primordial belief of theophany is the keynote of various ritualistic arts, with Padayani emerging as a notable expression, particularly in Kerala.

Padayani, a sublime art form, evolved in connection with the cult of the Mother Goddess. In Kerala, it was associated with the worship of Bhagavathi. Originating in Central Travancore, it later became popular in other states too. This art form tells the story of how Bhadrakali,[1] the daughter of Lord Shiva, kills Darikan, the asura king. Even

---

[1]Goddess Bhagavathi, a manifestation of Goddess Shakti, commands profound reverence in Kerala's temples with dedicated shrines found throughout the state. Regarded as the benevolent virgin mother, Bhagavathi also takes on the fierce form of Bhadrakali when the need arises, particularly to vanquish demons.

after the death of King Darikan, the fury of Bhadrakali does not subside until Murukan, son of Lord Shiva, creates intricate art using vibrant natural resources, ultimately appeasing Bhadrakali with his aesthetic art.

When Panicker was a child, he used to visit the Bhagavathi temple situated near his home, which exposed him to Padayani, a fusion of martial and aesthetic art forms that is performed at the Bhagavathi temple for a period of 24 days.[2] Everyone, regardless of religion and caste, takes part in Padayani. It symbolizes a remarkable human assembly characterized by tolerance and fraternity. Panicker drew inspiration from Padayani's aesthetic experience and interiorized the importance of fighting against evil to establish righteousness and justice in society. He assimilated the symbolic and metaphoric message of Padayani to substantiate the work of universalizing reading. Initially a one-man army, he was later joined by numerous people. The task of building a reading centre in his native place became a prestigious endeavour and Panicker accomplished it with grace. P.N. Panicker's humane nature won over the hearts of his fellow villagers, who found in him a visionary, a human symbol of renunciation and creativity. His love for exploration, learning, journey, thinking, experimentation and fostering human connections

---

[2]Padayani is performed from the middle of September to the middle of October (Kanni Masam as per the Malayalam calender).

regardless of religion, class, caste and language captivated the souls of the people, and they unconditionally hailed him as an angelic figure.

In his adolescent years, Panicker used to sit and chat with his acquaintances around a big bodhi (fig) tree (aalthara). It is believed that Gautama Buddha had attained enlightenment when he was meditating under a sacred fig, and Panicker also experienced his enlightenment in a similar setting. He put across the idea of forming a reading centre in his hometown to his friends. Although many worldly individuals assembled there regularly to discuss various subjects and also enjoyed themselves, most of the people who assembled were illiterate and impoverished. Realizing the predicament, Panicker zealously took up the task of introducing a newspaper for the first time in the village. His attempt to bring a newspaper to his panchayat marked the commencement of the people's library and literacy movements in Kerala.

Panicker was the cynosure of a united and cohesive community. His lovable and spirited nature captivated people who found in him a rare spark and an inexhaustible fire to enlighten generations. His unyielding efforts to bring newspapers from outside became successful. Thus, the residents of Neelamperoor gained access to newspapers like the *Malayala Manorama* and *Samadarshi*. Eventually the natives of Neelamperoor began to think about an urgent matter that concerned them—building a secure space for reading newspapers.

It was the Devaswom[3] of the Bhagavathi temple that fulfilled Panicker's dream of establishing a permanent reading house in the village. The Devaswom contributed a piece of land. The reading centre put up by Panicker offered the villagers a place to assemble for reading, exchanging ideas and indulging in discussions regarding social matters.

Panicker at that time had many personal interactions with veteran figures like K.C. Mammen Mappilai, the founder of *Malayala Manorama*, one of the leading newspapers in Malayalam, and Changanassery Parameswaran Pillai, the central committee member of the Harijan Seva Sangh. Panicker, being a leading cultural figure, had direct contact with many famous leaders like E.M.S., Panampilly Govinda Menon, C. Achutha Menon, P.K. Vasudevan Nair, R. Sankar, C.H. Mohammed Koya, K. Karunakaran, Joseph Mundassery (an outstanding literary critic) and C. Kesavan.

The memoirs and anecdotes written by several luminaries about P.N. Panicker are the most authentic sources of information that help us to understand how Panicker passionately waged a war against illiteracy and ignorance, which soon began to spread across India. Justice V.R. Krishna Iyer, A.K. Antony, Sukumar

---

[3]Devaswom are socio-religious trusts in India that manage and administer Hindu temples and their assets.

Azhikode, Professor S. Guptan Nair, M.P. Appan, Neelamperoor Madhusoodanan Nair, K. Chandrasekharan, K. Raman Pillai, M.K. Muneer, P.K. Narayana Pillai, D.C. Kizhakemuri, Thengamam Balakrishnan, Professor P. Meerankutty, I.V. Das, Dr V.S. Sharma, P.K. Warrier, T.N. Jayachandran, Dr Vellayani Arjunan, Manayath Chandran, Dr Vilakkudi Rajendran, Sukumaran Nair, Dr Ezhumattoor Rajaraja Varma, Dr Ambalapuzha Gopakumar, K. Sivadasan Pillai, K.G. Chellappan Pillai, Sreedharan Koyilandi, Namboothiri, K.S. Kuttappan Ambalappuzha, T.V. Gopalakrishnan, M.T. Vasudevan Nair, Dr M.R. Thampan and N. Balagopal (P.N. Panicker's son and head of the P.N. Panicker Foundation) are the veteran writers who wrote reminiscences apropos of the life, time and genius of Panicker.

One of the most passionate and lovely reminiscences is given by N. Balagopal, the beloved son of P.N. Panicker, in his article titled, 'Aarudeyum Vidheyathwathinu Adimappedatha Jeevitham' (The Life Not Subjugated to Anybody)[4]:

> When I recall Father, some events related to my career appear in my mind. From childhood itself it was my

[4]Balagopal, N., 'Aarudeyum Vidheyathwathinu Adimappedatha Jeevitham', *P. N. Panicker - Karmaveeryathinte Thejas*, Dr M.R. Thampan and Pattom G. Ramachandran Nair (eds), P.N. Panicker Foundation, Thiruvananthapuram, 2010.

ambition to become a doctor. While I was a child, I used to accompany my mother and sisters to the hospital. The doctor's coats, ties and stethoscopes as well as their overall demeanour mesmerized me. Besides this, my interaction with the family of my beloved friend, Dr Krishnananda Pai, also fostered my ambition. Dr K. Narayana Pai was an eminent doctor in Kerala and also a nationally recognized doctor, who was hailed as a people's doctor. Dr Krishnananda Pai was the elder son of Dr Narayana Pai. But Krishnananda had a severe disease called haemophilia, an incurable disease. At the age of forty-seven, my intimate friend departed from this world. I had been maintaining extremely friendly relations with Krishnananda since we were in class seven. Due to his health problems, we spent most of our time in the Pai household, learning and playing together, and coming into contact with the doctors who visited his house, which in turn intensified my aspiration to pursue medical education.

Moreover, my performance in the ESLC exam with flying colours and the consequent government scholarship had increased the possibility of getting admission to the medical course. After school education from Model School, Trivandrum, Krishnananda and I continued our studies together at Mar Ivanios College. We were enrolled in the second group of the first pre-degree course. My father disliked my education in the private college. But he went along as he was aware of the intense relationship between me and Krishnananda. However, in the final pre-degree exam, we didn't get the marks required for medical admission. It was contrary to our expectations. 'It frustrated me', said Jayanthi Pai, wife of Dr Pai, fully aware of our relationship. She always treated me with deep love and affection, as if I also were her son. In motivating and promoting me in my studies she was in the forefront. I was a part and parcel of her family interactions and was present in all their family functions.

Dr K.N. Pai, under the pressure of Jayanthi Pai's persuasion, helped me to attain a medical seat in the management quota. I hurried to my house to convey the glad news. My mother, Chempakakutty Amma, my brother and sisters rejoiced at the news. But my father, who was strict in life, didn't accede to the idea of seeking admission for his son by paying a huge sum of money. I was exhausted with frustration and pain. And we had no financial support to afford the capitation fee. In fact, while my father was working towards the betterment of society, we lost possession of my mother's ancestral home.

A man who was the paragon of sacrifice lived by renouncing

pleasures and possessions only for the betterment of a society living in the darkness of illiteracy, ignorance and slavery. He ignited the dreams of society and safeguarded the divine light of wisdom and knowledge. The saga of his life was as rhapsodic as the heroic epics and it was not free from tears and turmoil. When we dive into the details of his life depicted by biographers, we will get a vivid vision of a social activist who was extremely optimistic and deeply passionate, driven by an unknown ecstasy.

SANATHANA DHARMA VAYANASALA (THE READING HOUSE)

The name of the reading house is significant. The terms 'Dharma' and 'Sanathana' have philosophic connotations; the former indicates righteousness in thought, words and duties, and the latter connotes the eternal, ultimate or persistent. The name of the reading house exemplifies the goal of Panicker. The reading house built in his village was the debut of his endeavour to organize a library movement that had a mass following. Panicker worked relentlessly from dawn to dusk, traversing the diverse landscapes of Kerala—from slums and outskirts to hamlets, hilly lands, countryside and big cities—as a one-man missionary. He was like a persistent wind that blew not to extinguish light and fire but to spread it.

During the early period of his social work, P.N. Panicker

was assisted by the well-known Gandhian Changanassery Parameswaran Pillai. He was a social activist, judge, lawyer, attorney general and former president of the Nair Service Society. Pillai was a member of the Sree Moolam Popular Assembly and actively supported Panicker's mission to establish a reading house in Neelamperoor. Widely referred to as 'Changanassery', Pillai had a close relationship with Gandhi; like barrister G.P. Pillai, he too attracted the attention of Gandhi.

Panicker collected books from the houses in his village and stored them in the reading centre. According to Panicker, books were the best medicines for the mind. Following the debut experiment of the Sanathana Dharma reading house, he dedicated more than 30 years to the library movement, spreading the message of reading and writing.

Ananth Krishna, a journalist, recalls P.N. Panicker as follows[5]:

> Kerala's achievements in the social sector have long been celebrated with many proposing the 'Kerala Model' of development as an alternative to the 'Gujarat Model'. Kerala has no 'model' to speak of.

---

[5]Krishna, Ananth, 'How P N Panicker Single-Handedly Transformed Kerala's Literacy Landscape', *Swarajyamag*, 27 December 2017, https://swarajyamag.com/ideas/how-p-n-panicker-single-handedly-transformed-keralas-literacy-landscape. Accessed on 4 January 2024.

> However, this does not mean that we are to dismiss the gains that Kerala has made as an anomaly. There are certainly lessons that other states can learn from the Kerala experiment.
>
> Kerala's foremost achievement that must be celebrated is 100 per cent literacy. Investments in the education sector as the primary sector have not helped, but the activities and achievements of Puthuvayil Narayana Panicker, a former schoolteacher, should not be overlooked. It was under his leadership that a collective of libraries then functioning in the Kingdom of Travancore came together to form the 'All Travancore Grandhasala Sangham' or Travancore Library Association in 1945. The Association eventually transformed into the 'Kerala Grandhasala Sangham (KGS)'. This state-wide library movement worked to increase the reach and use of libraries, highlighting the importance of literacy, especially in the rural areas. This article highlights the contribution of this selfless voluntary organization and its tireless leader, whose contribution should not be lost to the sands of time, and should act as a pathway for other states to replicate Kerala's success.

P.N. Panicker was an emblematic figure who added to the legacy of luminaries such as Thunchaththu Ramanujan Ezhuthachan, acknowledged as the father of the Malayalam language; Shankaracharya, the great philosopher of Advaitha; Narayana Guru, etc. Panicker became the 'Father of the Library Movement in Kerala' by recognizing and building upon their contributions to cultural spheres. The honours and recognitions that Panicker attained, both within and outside the state, were from his debut mission—the Sanathana Dharma Reading House.

When he started the historic cultural centre, he was benevolently promoted by P. Madhavan Pillai, who was the then secretary of a cooperative enterprise situated at Neelamperoor. He was also a relative. It was P. Madhavan Pillai who motivated Panicker to read the *Swadeshabhimani* (The Patriot), which was a historically significant newspaper founded by Vakkom Mohammed Abdul Khader (1873–1932), popularly known as Vakkom Moulavi, a celebrated social reformer, prolific writer, Muslim scholar and freedom fighter from Travancore. K. Ramakrishna Pillai (1878–1916) was the editor of the newspaper. His criticism of the Diwan of Travancore, P. Rajagopalachari, and the Maharaja led to the eventual confiscation of the newspaper and Ramakrishna Pillai was arrested and exiled from Travancore. *Karl Marx*, the first-ever biography of Karl Marx in an Indian language, was written by him.

The habit of reading in Panicker was fostered by P. Madhavan Pillai, who contributed a stock of books owned by the cooperative enterprise (Sahakarana Sangham). That was the capital of the Sanathana Dharma Reading House.

Karuvanoor Ramachandran provides us short glimpses of the emblematic posture of P.N. Panicker through numerous articles published in prominent Malayalam media outlets such as *Kerala Kaumudi,* the leading daily; *Kalakaumudi,* a progressive weekly magazine; and other notable weeklies like *Mathrubhumi, Keralasabdam* and *Madhyamam.*

4
THE FAMILY MAN

One of the most beautiful and significant events in the life of P.N. Panicker was his marriage with Chempakakutty Amma of Aamayida Maliyekkal Parambil in 1930. Chempakakutty Amma, hailing from the Ambalappuzha district, was a pious and modest woman deeply rooted in the spiritual culture of Hinduism, especially acquired from epics like the *Mahabharata* and the *Ramayana*. She belonged to an affluent agrarian family and her parents possessed substantial property in their village.

As the spouse of an extraordinary social activist of punctilious convictions, Chempakakutty Amma had to live a life filled with challenges as her life partner, an ardent follower of Gandhian ideals, was never a full-time breadwinner of the family. Chempakakutty Amma had to shoulder much of the responsibility of the family herself. This does not mean that her husband neglected his responsibilities. Panicker was a loving husband and a caring father who managed the family while also moulding his children and wife apropos of the principles of Gandhian thought.

Throughout the challenging journey of life, the couple, along with their children, had to encounter countless pains and turmoil and supress many aspirations of their own. But they survived and overcame all their predicaments through the conscientious observance of right means and the virtuousness of leading a life uncontaminated by the temptations that often infiltrate the fabric of social life.

Chempakakutty Amma and Panicker had seven children—five daughters and two sons. The eldest daughter was Chandramathikutty, followed by Leela Kumari, Vilasinikutty, Indirakutty and Sumangaladevi. The sons were named Balagopal and Krishnakumar. N. Balagopal, the elder son of Panicker, continues to uphold the mission of his father as the vanguard of the P.N. Panicker Foundation. N. Balagopal writes[6]:

> ...an industrialist from Kottayam visited me. He promised me to make necessary arrangement for getting a medical admission for me at the Alappuzha Medical College on the condition that I marry his daughter after my studies. Knowing this, my father became furious. He convinced me that under any

[6]Balagopal, N., 'Aarudeyum Vidheyathwathinu Adimappedatha Jeevitham', *P.N. Panicker – Karmaveeryathinte Thejas,* Dr M.R. Thampan and Pattom G. Ramachandran Nair (eds), P.N. Panicker Foundation, Thiruvananthapuram, 2010.

> circumstance he would not let me live by surrendering to others. Consequently, there were some disputes in the family. My father was not ready to compromise on his tough stance. Though I was furious and angry with my father, I became conscious that his decision was appropriate and reasonable. Father was particularly diligent in following the principles in life that he professed on public platforms.
>
> I got admission for B.Sc. at University College, Trivandrum, and Father communicated all matters and the circumstances which led to my admission there with Dr N.S. Warrier, the then Principal of the college. He also requested the principal to provide me with sufficient guidelines. The principal had always inquired about my studies.

N. Balagopal's insightful reflection carries a profound message for future generations. It prompts individuals to appreciate and understand the resolute yet honest decisions made by parents that are rooted in integrity and devoid of corruption. The narrative serves as a beacon, guiding those who may feel frustrated momentarily by their parents' strictness, towards recognizing that these decisions were driven by righteous ideals rather than harshness. They will also recognize that such parents were their best allies rather than just 'loving' parents, steering their children away from the potential pitfalls of seeking favours rooted in emotional temperament, which may become the wrong path for both parents and children. There are many instances of this in our society where great men commit significant mistakes. In this context, the memoirs of N. Balagopal can serve as textbook for students. In today's social scenario, we frequently witness parents rushing into the pursuit of various enticing things to satisfy their children's desires, a tendency that leads to tragic and unnecessary outcomes.

Renowned Malayalam literary critic and orator Sukumar Azhikode gives an exciting account of the life of P.N. Panicker[7]:

> The people of Kerala always utter the epitomes given by some persons—Thunchaththu, Narayana Guru, Asan, etc. It is not easy to inscribe in the hearts of men. Similar words that resound in us are 'read and grow' given by P.N. Panicker. If the differences like caste and religion cease to exist and instead emerges a lovely humankind, it would be a creation of a posterity that grew out of reading.

---

[7]Azhikode, Sukumar, 'Panickarude Vazhi—The Pathway of Panicker', *P. N. Panicker—Karmaveeryathinte Thejas,* Dr M.R. Thampan and Pattom G. Ramachandran Nair (eds), P.N. Panicker Foundation, Thiruvananthapuram, 2010.

THE STRUGGLES OF LIFE

There were various ordeals in P.N. Panicker's life. While no one can be compared to another in either words or actions, parallels can be drawn between the lives of Panicker and P. Krishna Pillai in terms of their struggles, hard experiences and, above all, the triumph and journey of life. The latter was a prominent figure in the communist movement in Kerala. After completing basic education, Krishna Pillai turned to nationalist–social reformist endeavours and later became a stalwart of the communist movement. Like Panicker, he traversed every nook and corner of the state to build up the communist party. Both Krishna Pillai and Panicker embraced lives of simplicity and sacrifice.

Panicker's biographer, Pattom G. Ramachandran Nair in his book *P.N. Panicker* (in Malayalam)[8] writes:

> Dr Balan, Sangham worker and a close associate and relative of Panicker, wrote an article in May 1995 titled 'The Time that Can't be Forgotten'.
>
> 10 May was 'Valiyaperunnal, day, a public holiday. That day, Panicker had no public programmes. He made me write many letters to ministers and important persons; in between he got angry and

[8] *P. N. Panicker—Karmaveeryathinte Thejas*, Dr M.R. Thampan and Pattom G. Ramachandran Nair (eds), P.N. Panicker Foundation, Thiruvananthapuram, 2010.

> scolded me. The scolding ceased instantly. On one occasion, sir vehemently said, 'Balan's spouse died. She was so good. My spouse also died.' When he said this his eyes were filled with tears and his lips were trembling. We wept together; we were unable to speak for a while. This incident overwhelmed me. After completing the work, I accompanied him on his return journey. Letting him travel by himself, I thought, was not correct. There was a heavy downpour en route. The journey exhausted him and we reached Thiruvananthapuram. After handing him over to his son, Balagopal, I had returned. As I bid farewell, I never thought that it was to be his last journey to Kozhikode.

When dissatisfied with the familial atmosphere, Panicker used to meditate, often seeking solace in the serene sanctorum of the Neelamperoor shrine where he believed his Mother Goddess dwelt. The neighbourhood of the shrine held immense allure for a pious devotee. Panicker would express great enthusiasm and joy when talking about his beloved Goddess. According to the distinguished orator Sukumar Azhikode, Panicker must have been the perennial favourite of Saraswati, the deity of learning and knowledge. What Azhikode meant was that Panicker's entire life was dedicated to the pursuit of knowledge and literature. He was not only an excellent social organizer, inspiring a vast population for the cause of mass education and literacy, but also an outstanding orator who captivated audiences with his simple yet charming presentation of the subject. His speeches called for literacy and a renaissance in life, making him an exceptional figure in society. In a society marred by bruised egos and eccentric one-upmanship that disregard social progress and social peace, Panicker's meaningful speeches across the state differed from the moral posturing of deceptive and hypocritical politicians. He was well aware of the fact that women's empowerment would be incomplete without access to libraries; he conducted hundreds of pedestrian marches (padayatras) across the state to promote women's empowerment and universal literacy.

One of the most impactful campaigns led by P.N. Panicker was against the dowry system. He persuaded many women to pledge against dowry, recognizing it as an inhuman practice. He also appealed to both women and men to reject ostentatious weddings. Extravagant weddings, which are common in our society, driven by false pride and a desire to showcase social status, was seen by Panicker as a manifestation of egocentric fallacy and a hindrance to genuine social progress. This acts as a bottleneck to the harmonious development of society. Many impoverished social classes, despite being unable to afford the high expenses of a wedding, are forced to yield to social pressures and end up incurring debts to moneylenders.

As a consequence, many families find themselves pressured into relocating to slums on the outskirts of big cities. The distressing news of group suicides further intensified Panicker's resolve to combat these social evils and advocate leading a simple life. His commitment to a modest lifestyle and aversion to extravagance were such that he went to the extent of advising his daughters to refrain from wearing gold ornaments. While his resolute stance on this matter might have been misunderstood by his daughters as an expression of stubbornness and obstinacy, it reflected Panicker's prophetic and pragmatic approach to social reform. Panicker harboured a noble vision, a dream that almost all great humanists shared. This dream was to bring about an egalitarian and harmonious society based on religious tolerance and love.

In this respect, Panicker can be hailed as the 'Prometheus of India'. Aeschylus, in his ancient Greek tragedy, portrays Prometheus as the proto-martyr of freedom and knowledge. The myth of Prometheus, as written by Aeschylus in his play *Prometheus Bound*, revolves around the Titan Prometheus who defies Zeus, the king of the gods, by giving fire and knowledge to humanity. In Aeschylus' version, Prometheus steals fire from the gods and gifts it to humans, enabling them to progress in civilization. This act angers Zeus who then proceeds to punish Prometheus severely. He is bound to a rock, and an eagle sent by Zeus feeds daily on his liver, which regenerates everyday miraculously. Despite the suffering, Prometheus remains defiant in the face of adversity.

The legendary tale of Prometheus is metaphorically significant in relation to the life of P.N. Panicker because he, during his long battle against illiteracy and ignorance, had to undergo severe hardships in his life. Panicker worked tirelessly for his ultimate goal of universal literacy. He firmly believed that universal education was more important than universal suffrage. Without universal education, democracy would degenerate. But while he was immersed in his cause, his family life suffered due to acute financial difficulties.

Chempakakutty Amma, as I have already mentioned, hailed from a rich family of Ambalappuzha. Panicker, after marrying Chempakakutty Amma, had to live in her house as there was no male member to take care of the family. Therefore, after marriage, Ambalappuzha became the theatre of Panicker's social activities.

Being a full-time social activist, Panicker was busy with organizational work, leaving the burden of household activities on Chempakakutty Amma. Their home was frequently visited by noteworthy individuals, making it a bustling place, and Chempakakutty Amma, with remarkable commitment and confidence, handled various duties. Similar to Kasturba Gandhi, who lived and worked hard alongside Gandhi ji, Chempakakutty Amma fulfilled the domestic responsibilities of the family. She was a fountain of affection, love, commitment and confidence. As a result of a cardiac arrest, she departed from this world around 8.30 p.m. on 25 July 1991. Her sudden demise affected Panicker profoundly. He lost not only his life partner but also his inspiration and an inexhaustible source of energy.

It is important to bear in mind that the demise of Chempakakutty Amma was not the first tragedy that Panicker had to endure. It was the second—the first being the unexpected loss of his youngest daughter, Geetha Kumari, when she was just a student, studying in seventh standard at Cotton Hill School. The incident took place on 13 November 1968 and shattered the whole family. It is said that gastroenteritis (an inflammation of the stomach and intestines) took away her young life. In her memory, Panicker instituted the Geetha Memorial Award for girls who scored the highest marks in the seventh standard at the Cotton Hill Girls High School, Thiruvananthapuram.

Panicker's entire life stands as a valuable guide for future generations as it provides ethical guidelines for moralities derived not from any religious texts but from the divine lives of remarkable individuals like Gandhi, Narayana Guru and Mother Teresa. In every aspect of his personal life, Panicker remains a role model for posterity. His wealth was not measured by his bank balance—as he had no material possessions—but by his great work for universal education. For more than three decades he was the head of the library movement in Kerala and worked without remuneration. Such a man is rare to find in the present era.

5

THE P.K. MEMORIAL READING HOUSE

Ambalappuzha has long been known as the cradle of cultural activities. The cultural heritage and legacy of Amabalappuzha inspired Panicker to launch an epoch-making experiment of establishing a reading house there. He commenced the mission in a rented space by convening a meeting of eminent personalities at the reading centre. The reading house was launched in memory of P.K. Narayana Pillai, a native of Ambalappuzha and a judge of the High Court of Kerala, better known as Sahitya Panchanan—a celebrated critic of Malayalam literature. P.K. Narayana Pillai was also called 'Nirupaka Kesari'—the king of literary critics. Earlier named P.K. Vilasam Vayanasala, the name of the reading house was changed to P.K. Memorial Grandhasala after Pillai's death on 10 February 1936. Panicker worked as the secretary of the reading house with P.K. Madhavakuruppu serving as the president. P.K. Memorial Grandhasala heralded the formation of the Grandhasala movement in Kerala.

The P.K. Vilasam Library was built in 1936. A close associate of Panicker in this venture was Karur Karayil Sivarama Pillai, who was a painter and teacher. Unfortunately, the reading house could continue for only six months as the organizers of the reading house were unable to sustain its working. At that time, Panicker was transferred from Neelamperoor to Ambalappuzha as a teacher and took charge of the primary school in Ambalappuzha.

P.K. Vilasam Library was renamed P.K. Vilasam Vayanasala by Panicker in August 1937. K.K. Kunju Pillai, a well-known freedom fighter, was another personage who worked at the vayanasala during its initial stages. Along with him, there were veteran organizers like G.N. Nair, K.C. Kesava Pillai, Damodara Kaimal, Madhava Kurup, M.R. Chellappan Pillai and Narayana Pillai.

The librarian was Necheri Karunakaran who later joined the police department and was promoted to Circle Inspector. P. Kunhan Kurup granted 10 cents of land free of cost, enabling the library to function independently. Sardar K.M. Panikkar, V. Krishnan Thampi, K.G. Parameswaran Pillai, C. Achutha Menon, Dr Sooranad P. N. Kunjan Pillai and Malloor Govinda Pillai were some famous people who visited the library. The great Malayalam poet Vallathol Narayana Menon also visited the library in 1942. The poet wrote in the visitors' diary as follows:

1117, Meenam 25th, one of the good days in my life; it is on this day I saw the P.K. Memorial Library, a sight that was gratifying to my eyes. The reading house situated beside the Ambalappuzha Parthasarathi Temple is adorned with diverse and divine books; a suitable building is also being constructed for it. Thus, when it is shifted to a pure and broad building, it will enlighten excellently, viewed excellently, serve excellently as the river Ganga and the library will always be like Haridwar. God, advisor of the quintessence of the Upanishad, Parthasarathy, thy merciful blessing may fall upon the asylum of knowledge, which commemorates Sahitya Panchanan.

THE ORIGIN OF THE GRANDHASALA SANGHAM

The inception of the Grandhasala Sangham was a milestone in the history of the library movement in Kerala. It was in 1945 that the Travancore Grandhasala Sangham was established under the leadership of P.N. Panicker. Simultaneously, there was also a library movement in Cochin (now Kochi) under the leadership of M.K. Raja, known as the 'Akhila Cochi Grandhasala Sangham'. In Malabar, K. Kelappan, also known as 'Kerala Gandhi,' spearheaded a library organization. Following the merger of Travancore and Cochin states, the Travancore Grandhasala Sanghom transformed into the Thiru–Kochi Grandhasala.

Finally, by merging the three library organizations in 1956, the Kerala Grandhasala Sangham came into being with Trivandrum (now Thiruvananthapuram) as its headquarters.

K.S. Ranjith, in his discussion paper,[9] writes:

> The changing character of the library movement and its organizational efforts were seen more in Travancore. The library organizations formed in this region tried to please the colonial rulers, primarily with the objective of securing funds. This was evident from the proceedings of the first conference of Travancore Grandhasala Sangham. The diwan of Travancore, Sir C.P. Ramaswamy Iyer, inaugurated the conference held at PKM Library in Ambalappuzha on 16 September 1945. Although he was an administrator with sound views on the developmental needs of the state, he was an infamous dictator who had taken severe steps for suppressing people's movement. So he was very unpopular among the radicals of the state. Thus, there was a difference of opinion about inviting him for the inauguration of the library conference. But the dominant group under the leadership of P.N. Panicker succeeded in their attempts to ensure the diwan's participation in the library conference, in which 47 libraries in Travancore participated. This meeting and

---

[9]Ranjith, K.S., 'Discussion Paper No. 78, Rural Libraries of Kerala', *Kerala Research Programme on Local Level Development Centre for Development Studies*, 2004.

> the formation of Travancore Grandhasala Sangham was the first step towards a democratic institution of the apex body of the libraries.
>
> The role of P.N. Panicker in organizing a library network in the state deserves special mention. He was associated in the formation of Sanathana Dharma Vayanasala in Neelamperoor, Alappuzha. He succeeded in getting a grant of ten rupees from the government for this library. He realized that the government and the official agencies have to play an important role in promoting the library movement and secured all possible assistance from them in forming (and reviving) rural libraries. He devoted his time entirely for the cause of the library movement in Kerala.

The aforesaid observation of K.S. Ranjith is an appropriate tribute to P.N. Panicker. What Panicker founded in Kerala was not merely reading houses where people sat, read and left but centres that served as dynamic universities of cultural interaction. Eminent littérateurs, social activists and cultural luminaries would assemble there for literary meetings, artistic events and literary programmes that were regularly organized.

The president of the Travancore Grandhasala Sangham was K.M. Kesavan with Panicker as the general secretary and Kesava Pillai as the treasurer. Panicker's work was not confined to a particular library and his responsibility extended to visiting the libraries in other places and addressing their grievances.

When C. Kesavan was the chief minister, he granted the Thulasi Hill building to the Grandhasala Sangham to use it as its office. There were more than 5,000 libraries in Kerala when they were merged into KGS. The Sangham was very vigilant in organizing literary seminars and other events to foster the aspirations of readers and writers. There were also writers' workshops conducted across the state. In northern Kerala, K. Kelappan, K.P. Kesava Menon and E.M.S. Namboodiripad were actively involved in promoting the library movement. When E.M.S. became the general secretary of the Kerala Pradesh Congress Committee, he introduced several measures that ensured the movement kept going. He issued a circular to carry out library work at the grassroots level in society. Rural libraries were envisioned as the focal point for the downtrodden who had long been subjected to severe exploitation and oppression by the dominant classes of society in the country.

P.N. Panicker visited homes to collect books and distributed these books to the libraries. At that time, the rural libraries in Kerala conducted evening and night classes to promote library usage. The libraries constructed in various parts of Kerala were also the centres of performing arts and literary functions. They served as platforms for inclusive and constructive discussions, transcending political, religious and other narrow differences. Specific programmes were developed to foster the involvement of women and children. At that time, the empowerment of women was a significant agenda of the Kerala Grandhasala Sangham as Panicker envisioned women's empowerment as a prerequisite for the liberation of society. He realized the fact that the crucial problem society faced was the mental enslavement of people. Panicker recognized the age-old male domination as a threat to freedom and saw the literacy movement as imperative for the emancipation of women. The library movement in Kerala also established nursery schools, known as Balakairali, which were a blessing to the underprivileged.

After the formation of the Kerala Grandhasala Sangham, rural and urban libraries sprang up extensively in every part of the state.

A. Paslithil in his book, *Public Library Movement: Kerala*,[10] states:

> The slumbering depressed communities gradually woke up through their own organizations, educational institutions, temples, libraries and industries. Popular socio-religious reform movements of the depressed communities played a vital role in the social reformation of Kerala. Social reform movement led by Narayana Guru (1854–1928), Chattampi

[10]Paslithil, A., *Public Library Movement: Kerala*, Kalpaz Publications, Delhi, 2006.

Swamikal (1853–1934), Ayyankali (1861–1941), Vaghbadananda (1885–1940) and A. Ayyappan (1889–1968) helped the people of Kerala to taste the sweetness of modern development.

The Grandhasala Sangham, under Panicker's able leadership, won the prestigious Nadezhda K. Krupskaya Prize (named after Lenin's wife) from UNESCO in 1975.

OPEN SPACE, OPEN DEBATE

Libraries are not only centres of public discourse but can also be utilized for developing civic consciousness as they provide sufficient space for the discussion of serious issues. P.N. Panicker led the library movement in Kerala to improve literacy in the state. During 1955–75, the Kerala State Library Council had a record of 8,417 libraries under it.

Panicker was an ardent advocate of the literacy movement in Kerala and laboriously attempted to awaken the civic consciousness of the people there. His efforts were directed towards the most alienated people of society, specifically women, children, the economically poor and socially oppressed classes. He aimed at the upliftment of the most exploited classes and empowering the masses. It was through the concerted efforts of Panicker that Kerala as a society became conscious of civil issues. The libraries established and reformed under the leadership of Panicker worked as the centres for addressing many major social issues like the environment, literacy and social awakening. His slogan of 'Read and Grow' was not an academic plan but rather a cultural tool for social liberation.

Historians have given due recognition to the significant contributions that Panicker carried out to the library movement and later the literacy movement. His life exemplified Ralph Waldo Emerson's observation that 'an institution is the lengthened shadow of one man.' Despite his frail appearance, Panicker's influence grew, making him a legend in his own lifetime and thereafter.

Many social activists were drawn to P.N. Panicker's influence. Madhuravanam Krishna Kurup, D.C. Kizhakemuri, Ulloor S. Parameswara Iyer, Rao Bahadur Professor K.V. Rangaswami Aiyangar, A.N. Thampi and K.G. Thomas were fascinated by Panicker's social commitment. He was the architect of the widely acclaimed 'Kerala Model' of development which went on to become an example for all other states in India and beyond. The celebrated Malayalam novelist Thakazhi Sivasankara Pillai hailed Panicker as the 'Cultural Father of Kerala', while Sukumar Azhikode placed him at the forefront when considering eminent personalities of Kerala.

The activities of the Kerala Grandhasala Sangham (Kerala State Library Council) ignited a popular cultural movement in Kerala at the end of which the state acquired total literacy in the 1990s. It was Panicker who carried the message of education and development even to the remotest corners and neglected tribal pockets of Kerala. Starting with 47 libraries in 1945, the Grandhasala Sangam grew into a network of more than 6,000 libraries spread across the towns and villages of Kerala. To provide this initiative a developmental structure, Panicker established KANFED. Together, these two associations transformed a mere initiative into a movement that profoundly impacted the education, culture and development of Kerala.

Professor G.N. Panicker in his article 'Samskarikam'[11] writes,

> We have around five thousand public libraries and hundreds of school/college libraries. All of them formed the heart of cultural activities. This period was the time of regular book reading, speeches and discussions on books. The communists, at that time, were fully involved with library activities, unaffected by the obsession of party politics. They attempted to organize all people under the flag of libraries and reading houses. Communists, at that time, were broad-minded people. They naturally adored libraries. They also respected the secretary of the Grandhasala Sangham. Eventually, the venom of

[11]Panicker, G.N., 'Samskarikam', *Aayirathi Ambathukalilum Arupathukalilum Nammude Grandhasalakal*, p. 57.

politicization affected the libraries, which gradually shattered them...

In 1963, K.A. Damodara Menon was elected the president of the Kerala Grandhasala Sangham. A prominent figure in the political sphere, he had served as the Minister of Industries in the cabinet of Pattom A. Thanu Pillai and R. Sankar. He was also the editor of the *Mathrubhumi Daily*. In 1965, P.C. George took over as the president of the Grandhasala Sangham. P.N. Panicker held the position of secretary of the Grandhasala Sangham for 32 years, marking a unique record in the organization.

Apart from his leadership role, Panicker was also a publisher who encouraged both young and veteran writers to publish their articles in the *Grandhalokam*, the journal of the Grandhasala Sangham. The journal commenced publishing under the auspices of the Thiru–Kochi Grandhasala Sangham. S. Guptan Nair, a well-known Malayalam critic, was the editor of *Grandhalokam*. The name 'Grandhalokam' is derived from the term 'Dhwanyaalokam', a concept believed to be attributed to Anandavardhana, a celebrated literary scholar of ancient India. 'Dhwanyaalokam' is a fusion of the words 'dhwani', representing the intonation or connotation of literature, and 'alokam', meaning light or perception. So the term 'Grandhalokam' was the most apt word to symbolize the enlightening role of books.

Several distinguished personalities contributed significantly to the library movement in Kerala. Vellayani Arjunan, the famous writer, was one of the organizers of the library movement who worked to resuscitate the libraries of Trivandrum. His effort to uplift the library missions at Neyyattinkara Taluk in Trivandrum deserves special mention. K. Damodaran, a distinguished Marxist theoretician and author, had also worked for the library movement in Kerala. N.V. Krishna Warrier, the famous Malayalam poet and literary figure (also the author of *Nannangadikal, Kochu Thoman* and *Africa* and director of the Kerala Bhasha Institute), S.K. Pottekkatt, Karimpuzha Ramakrishnan, Pavanan, Moyarath Sankaran, Kozhipurath Madhava Menon and M.K.K Nair are other remarkable names apropos the library movement who are to be specially mentioned here. T.N. Gopinathan Nair was another notable person who participated in the functioning of the library movement.

When the Grandhasala workers' meeting was held at the town hall in Calicut (or Kozhikode) on 11 June 1937, K. Kelappan presided over the session. This session facilitated the formation of the Akhila Malabar Vayanasala (All Malabar Reading House) and K. Damodaran was the convenor of the committee formed at the session.

Along with the library movement, P.N. Panicker also undertook several social ventures like blood donation movements, establishing prison libraries, visiting rescue homes and mental hospitals, school and college instruction classes, non-formal education movement, agrarian schemes and environment protection programmes.

Panicker, being a leading cultural figure, had direct contact with many famous leaders like E.M.S., Panampilly Govinda Menon, C. Achutha Menon, P.K. Vasudevan Nair, R. Sankar, C.H. Mohammed Koya, K. Karunakaran, Joseph Mundassery and C. Kesavan.

THE LIBRARY MAN

The Prophet of Islam, Muhammad Nabi, once said, 'Seek knowledge even if you have to go as far as China.' The very connotation of the word 'Quran' is 'to read'. Socrates, the ancient Greek philosopher and promoter of knowledge, emphasized the value of knowledge by asserting that 'The only good is knowledge and the only evil is ignorance.' Those who harbour hatred or fear towards knowledge are the forces of evil, personifying ignorance. P.N. Panicker's life was essentially an epitomization of these ideals of wisdom and knowledge. An admirer of Mahatma Gandhi, Panicker was inspired by the Gandhian philosophy that 'illiteracy is a curse and shame of the country and it should be wiped out as early as possible.' The political atmosphere of Kerala was favourable for setting up the most powerful voluntary organization of the people and Panicker succeeded in assimilating the right means fro Sri. m the cultural legacy of Kerala.

A. Paslithil in his book, *Public Library Movement: Kerala,*[12] observes:

> During this period, Kerala witnessed great socio-political developments. In addition to the social reforms mentioned earlier, the caste organizations and political parties like the *Sri. Narayana Dharma Paripalana Sanghom* (1903), *Yoga Kshema Sabha* (1908), *Nair Service Society* (1914) and the Indian National Congress and its regional leaders led the campaign for eradication of untouchability and other social evils [that] prevailed in the Society. These caste organisations declared war against some of the outdated social practices and pleaded the people to switch over to the track of modernism.

The major events in the agitation against untouchability were the Vaikom Satyagraha (1924–25) and the Guruvayur Satyagraha (1931–32). These movements gained nationwide attention and Mahatma Gandhi himself was involved in both. On 12 November 1936, the Maharaja of Travancore, Chithira Thirunal Balarama Varma, issued a historic proclamation, throwing open temples in Travancore to all Hindus irrespective of caste.

Simultaneously, a series of social regulation acts like the Nair Regulation Act of 1925, Cochin Nair Act of 1937–38

---

[12]Paslithil, A., *Public Library Movement: Kerala*, Kalpaz Publications, Delhi, 2006.

and Mappila Marumakkathayam Act of 1939 passed by the respective governments of Travancore, Cochin and Madras transformed the traditional joint family system by allowing the partition of the joint family (Tharavad) property. It also legalized the inheritance from father to son instead of uncle to nephew.

The introduction of land reforms in Kerala during this period paved the way for a new socio-economic order. Amendments to the Janmi-Kudiyan Regulation of 1932 by the Travancore government granted full property rights to kudiyans (tenants) subject to the payment of janmi karam (landlord's rent). The Tenancy Act of 1939 provided security of tenure and enabled aggrieved parties to approach courts of law for the determination of fair rent. The working class became more conscious of their rights and duties and they formed their own unions for collective bargaining. The working class in Alleppey (or Alappuzha) took the lead on this front by organizing a labour union on 31 March 1922. During 1934 and 1935, a series of industrial strikes took place in Cannanore (now Kannur), Calicut, Feroke, Trichur (now Thrissur), Cochin and Alleppey. These strikes played a pivotal role in organizing the working class of Kerala into cohesive groups.

There may be different opinions about hailing P.N. Panicker as the father of the library movement in Kerala. Those who are opposed to qualifying him as such argue that leaders existed in various parts of the state before

Panicker. The debate over whether P.N. Panicker should be hailed as the father of the library movement in Kerala is reminiscent of similar debates about figures like Mahatma Gandhi being called the father of the nation. When we hail Gandhi as the father of our nation, what we mean is that he was the foremost national leader who succeeded in awakening the vast majority of the population against British colonial rule.

It was Gandhi who aroused the cultural and political spirit of the people and instilled a sense of nationalism based on religious harmony and cultural heritage. Regarding the role of Panicker in the people's library movement of Kerala, one can undoubtedly say that he is the father of the library movement because it was he who unified the work of the library movement in Kerala, integrated their functioning, gave them far-sighted guidelines, introduced multifaceted projects and action plans and, above all, was responsible for giving the library movement a strong following of the people. In addition to all this, Panicker worked towards having a constitutional and legal foundation for the library movement in Kerala.

One of Panicker's significant achievements was securing financial grants from the government for the Grandhasala Sangham. According to the scheme of the government, all libraries in the state affiliated with the Sangham received financial aid. The second conference of the Grandhasala Sangham held at Kottayam in 1947 decided to extend its function to the field of literacy programmes throughout the state. The conference also decided to introduce legal protection for the library movement. In 1948, the Sangham created its manual, which outlined the objectives and programmes to be carried out across the state.

The third conference of the Sangham was held at Paravur on 15 and 16 July 1948. The session was presided over by Panampilly Govinda Menon, who later became the prime minister of Cochin state and had previously served as the president of the Grandhasala Sangham, contributing significantly to the library movement. The Sangham had also commenced a certificate course in Library Sciences.

Universal education and 100 per cent literacy were the two major goals of the Grandhasala Sangham. Without achieving these goals, the democratization and the material and cultural growth of society would have remained an utopian dream. Sooranad Kunjan Pillai, P.V. Ulahannan Pillai, Kainikkara Kumara Pillai and N. Gopala Pillai were some of the notable individuals who contributed to the library movement during this period. The aforesaid also served as members of the advisory board of the Sangham.

K.P. Vijayan, in his book *P.N. Panicker—Grandhasalayude Perunthachan*[13] says:

[13]Vijayan, K.P., *P.N. Panicker—Grandhasalayude Perunthachan*, Insight Publica, Kozhikode, 2006.

Panicker was able to make the changing governments understand the functioning of the Grandhasala Sangham and also to make them understand the imperative of facilitating the growth of the cultural movement. Panicker's aim was to tell the government to not ignore the Sangham. The Sangham had grown as the centre of power in the sphere of culture. On behalf of the silver jubilee of the Sangham, a cultural rally had started from the northern part of Kerala at the Kasaragod municipal library on 8 November 1970 and reached Trivandrum on 20 December. It is doubtful that such a rally, awakening the villages and cities of Kerala with the slogan 'read and grow' has been conducted anywhere in India. The chief minister and other ministers received the rally by raising slogans along with Panicker [...]

This was the first rally conducted in Kerala towards achieving a cultural and intellectual goal.

THE TRIVANDRUM PUBLIC LIBRARY

The Trivandrum Public Library was the first public library in Kerala, established during the period of Swathi Thirunal, the King of Travancore. The public library of Trivandrum was the cynosure of the city at that period. Even before the establishment of the public library, there was a reading house in Travancore at the Travellers Bungalow. Travancore rulers valued learning and reading as integral components of culture, so they stored many books, some of which had been written five or six centuries ago.

The library attracted visits from several world-famous personalities and was the first library to obtain government grants. Swathi Thirunal, who was a patron of art, literature and culture, gave a special grant of a thousand rupees to the library. The public library of Trivandrum became a registered society in 1847. In 1894, the society became a joint stock company and evolved into the Public Library Association. It was Moolam Thirunal, the then King of Travancore who opened the library for the common people in 1897. During that period, the library had many precious and valuable books that earned it academic and cultural prestige. The promoters of the library, including P.N. Panicker, had envisioned that the libraries should become not only reading centres but also houses of cultural activities and dreams.

Nowadays, our libraries are generally in a pathetic condition because the authorities concerned are found to be ignorant of the basic objectives of libraries. They have turned libraries into mute houses where readers are afraid to even inhale openly, fearing that they might break the imposed silence. Such conditions, characterized by extreme surveillance, excessive identification practices and harsh behaviour on the part of library officials were not expected and go against the very essence of what libraries should be. Even controversial rulers like C.P. Ramaswami Iyer recognized the importance of libraries, exempting them from autocracy and providing patronage. Libraries should have discipline but discipline should never be imposed arrogantly; instead, it has to be inspired naturally by the cultural atmosphere of the library. Libraries should become centres for debates and intellectual discussions rather than being places of surveillance and policing. Panicker's dream was to adapt the libraries to a new cultural scenario, as he had a humane attitude towards people.

P.N. Panicker had a profound vision for libraries, seeing them as agents of emancipation capable of liberating people from age-old social hierarchies, caste-based egoism, inferiority complexes (and its counterpart, megalomania), inhuman practices, etc. His deep social sense led him to advocate for the end of all kinds of bondages in society.

K.P. Vijayan, the biographer of P.N. Panicker, writes in his lucid style[14]:

> By his humble life and noble thoughts, Panicker became the elevated model of public service. In order to lead the country from darkness to light and from degeneration to regeneration, he

---

[14]Vijayan, K.P., *P.N. Panicker—Grandhasalayude Perunthachan*, Insight Publica, Kozhikode, 2006, 46.

> sacrificed his life. He was leading a fruitful and devoted life. His life was filled with hard work and experiments. He set aside life for an exclusive motto to inculcate letters and instil knowledge. He successfully completed the mission by agitating and fighting for long decades.

Under the leadership of the Grandhasala Sangham, there was a notable intellectual awakening in the rural communities of Kerala. This created lively and extensive debates on the burning issues that people faced in day-to-day life, and discussions began on the prevalent political and social issues at both national and international levels. The Sangham took an active part in organizing literary seminars and science exhibitions across the state. Awards were given to libraries for their functioning and performance. Prizes were also instituted for the best student reader in the state, thus motivating them—this is something that the present lot of libraries generally ignore.

As a result of some internal problems arising from political conflicts within the Sangham, the government had to take over its administration in 1977. This was during the last phase of the emergency period. Through an ordinance dated 16 March 1977 and Act No. 19 of 1977, the government appointed a control board and brought KGS under its authority. The names of the members of this board are given below:

1. Chakkeeri Ahamed Kutty (Chairman)
2. P.N. Panicker (Secretary)
3. N.V. Krishna Warrier
4. P.T. Bhaskara Panicker
5. Dr A.N.P. Ummerkutty
6. P. Chitran Namboodirippad
7. A. Balagopal
8. Finance Secretary (state government)

When the government took over the libraries in Kerala, a grading system was introduced based on which the libraries were given grants. The government categorized the libraries into eight grades and each grade was granted financial aid accordingly.

ENTERING THE LITERACY FIELD

P.N. Panicker donned many hats, namely, of a social activist, organizer, teacher and, above all, a cultural pioneer who worked tirelessly for the development of society. He, just like S.R. Ranganathan (father of Indian library science), fought against corruption, bureaucratic red-tapism, nepotism and other social evils. He was loved and respected widely in the state for his immense and unparalleled contributions to the library movement. According to Panicker, library work should have a deep and comprehensive world outlook to conceive social and cultural work as a theatre of liberating cultural actions. It was in this social context that Panicker, in the midst of his long and hard work encompassing the library movement, undertook the responsibility of the literacy movement in the state. Thus the Grandhasala Sangham turned its attention towards the literacy movement.

P.N. Panicker was well aware of the importance of universal free education and emerged as the pioneer of the literacy movement in Kerala, acting as its archangel. The entry of the Grandhasala Sangham into the literacy field was an epoch that heralded the dawn of the cultural awakening in Kerala. Panicker, known for his workaholic nature, dedicated himself to executing literacy programmes at the grassroots level.

It is estimated that more than 800 million people worldwide above the age of fifteen are illiterate. Panicker, recognizing the intricate interplay between educational and social contexts, comprehended the importance of focussing on literacy programmes. It was in this context that KANFED endorsed the movement launched by Panicker. The eminent people who worked with broad perspectives and determination were P.T. Bhaskara Panicker, K.M. Kesavan, P.T. Thomas, K.A. Damodara Menon, R. Sankar, Paravoor T.K., P.S. George and Thayatt Sankaran.

P.T. Bhaskara Panicker was the president of the Malabar District Board. Apart from being an eminent scientific litterateur who wrote profusely on different disciplines, he was also the chief editor of an encyclopaedia and undertook the publishing of its ten volumes. A versatile genius and a close associate of P.N. Panicker, he dedicated over 50 years in his attempt to rejuvenate both the library and literacy movements. He was also one of the chief ideologues of Marxism.

Under the collective leadership of P.N. Panicker and P.T. Bhaskara, the Grandhasala Sangham succeeded in building work-oriented literacy projects in Kerala and converted one lakh illiterates into literates. This was a brilliant era in which literacy programmes were commenced in more than 3,500 centres. G. Sankara Kurup, the eminent Malayalam poet, and Benedict Mar Gregorios were other outstanding figures who worked for the literacy programmes.

The 1970s saw the Grandhasala Sangham reach the zenith of its functioning. In 1971, C.H. Mohammed Koya, the education minister, presented Panicker a state car typically reserved for ministers. Panicker, being a staunch Gandhian, was unaffected by this act as he didn't even use ordinary cars. Koya persuaded him to use it, stating that people like Panicker had the moral authority to use such cars. Panicker was extremely idealistic in his outlook towards life, which reflected in his dress, food habits, travel choices and every sphere of life. He was a 'puritan' by morals and never spent public funds for personal needs.

One of the remarkable qualities of P.N. Panicker was his ability to unify different people under his exalted slogans of 'Read and Grow' and 'Think and Be Wise'. The eminent personalities who united under the library and literacy movements were E.M.S. Namboodiripad, A.K. Gopalan, P. Kesavadev, Dr P.K. Narayana Pillai, K.P. Kesava Menon, M.K.K. Nair, Abdurrahiman Bafaqi Thangal, K.M. Mathew, K. Sukumaran, T.N. Jayachandran Nair, Professor P. Gopala Pillai, Sooranad Kunjan Pillai, Dr K. Raghavan Pillai, K.P.R. Rayarappan, V.R. Krishnan Ezhuthachan, Chowara Parameswaran, P.K. Vasudevan Nair, V.M.M. Nair, E. Ikkanda Warrier, Father Vadakkan, U.A. Beeran, N. Sreekantan Nair, Pirappancode Murali, K. Karunakaran, K.P. Madhavan Nair, J. Rajagopalan Nair, Veli Krishnan Nair, Kesava Pillai, Thathamathu Nanu, Sivan Pillai, V.G. Panicker, Advocate P. Kunjarama Kuruppu, Advocate P. Parameswaran Pillai and I.V. Das. Among these notable names was I.V. Das, a close associate of Panicker who played a significant role in leading the Grandhasala Sangham for many years.

C. Achutha Menon, the then chief minister of Kerala, was fascinated by the industrious and dedicated life of Panicker. During the literacy movement, when Prime Minister Morarji Desai emphasized the need for a district action plan, a comprehensive literacy programme for the entire nation was devised. In order to achieve the goal, the prime minister convened a special conference at Delhi where Justice V.R. Krishna Iyer, P.N. Panicker and M.D. Nalapat participated as delegates from Kerala. The prime minister praised Panicker's mission and handed over the literacy programme of Kerala to KANFED.

The Grandhasala Sangham elected P.N. Panicker as the general secretary in 1945, a post he held till 1977. The presidency of the Grandhasala Sangham was held by distinguished individuals such as K.M. Kesavan, P.T. Thomas, Paravoor T.K., Panampilly Govinda Menon, K.A. Damodara Menon, R. Sankar, P.S. George, P.T. Bhaskara Panicker and Thayatt Sanakaran. When the administration of the Sangham came under the control board during the elections in 1973, Panicker served as the first member secretary of the control board.

A noteworthy project undertaken by Panicker was the protection of nature and the environment. In order to fulfil this goal, he instituted a forestation action plan. He staunchly opposed deforestation and urged to inculcate the necessity of protecting the environment and ecology in students and youngsters. He stressed the inevitability of environmental studies in the curriculum.

Panicker was committed to the emancipation of women, Dalits and Adivasis. He founded the Kerala Educational Development and Employment Society (KEDES), an organization aimed at the fulfilment of Gandhian precepts and the empowerment of women and Dalits through employment. Under the leadership of Justice V.R. Krishna

Iyer as the president and M.M. Thomas as the working president of the organization, small manufacturing units were established in the villages of Kollam, Neyyattinkara, etc. The organization also successfully experimented with the use of solar energy in rural areas. In many ways, Panicker emerged as an unwavering advocate for social justice, embodying deep human love.

One of the inspiring writers and ideologues of Marxism, P. Govinda Pillai writes[15]:

> The enviable and somewhat astonishing growth of Kerala was not born at once nor was it an accidental event. From Narayana Guru to Ayyankali's Sadhu Jana Paripalana Sangham communist movement, to movements like the United Political Nivarthana Uprising of the 1930s and the National Sahacharya Movement, and from Aikya Kerala Prasthanam and the first public library of Swathi Thirunal to the Grandhasala Sangham of P.N. Panicker and ten other veteran persons—all played a historic role in actualizing the Kerala Model. It was in this scenario that P.N. Panicker also embellished the row of the rchitects of Kerala.

All through the 1970s and 1980s Panicker strived to attain the goals that the constitution of our nation emphasizes,

[15]Pillai, P. Govinda, and K.P. Vijayan. 'Mannil Ninnuyarnnu Vanna Mahameru', *P.N. Panicker—Grandhasalayude Perunthachan*, Insight Publica, Kozhikode, 2006.

embodying the spirit of a committed missionary tirelessly advocating for libraries. I do not mean that Panicker was not backed by anyone in his tasks, but what we have to bear in mind is that while he was assisted by many significant people in his attempts, there was not sufficient material and financial resources for the fulfilment of the objectives of the Grandhasala Sangham. The foundational projects, conceptualization, the long-term projects, action plans, paradigms related to strategies and practices were not undertaken by the governments or by any single authority. In navigating these challenges, Panicker has left an indelible mark on history.

Being a gifted public speaker, Panicker captivated, motivated and mobilized people to achieve the noble ideals of cultural growth and social development. He persuaded them to fight against communalism, illiteracy, chauvinism, corruption, nepotism and moral decay. His life was an elevated example of righteousness and furthered the enlightened mission of renaissance. He rightly deserves to be hailed as the father of the cultural renaissance of Kerala.

Prime Minister Narendra Modi interacting with N. Balagopal, vice chairman of the P.N. Panicker Foundation, and other functionaries of the Foundation during the 22nd Reading Day-Reading Month celebrations held on 17 June 2017. Influenced by the interaction, PM Modi spoke about books in 'Mann ki Baat' soon after the event.

'Present a book instead of a bouquet in all public functions'
—PM Modi in 'Mann ki Baat' episode, 25 June 2017

Subsequent to PM's 'Mann ki Baat' programme, the Ministry of Home Affairs, Government of India, had issued directions to all Central and State Government departments, institutions, public sector enterprises, etc., to adopt the practice of the P.N. Panicker Foundation of presenting a book instead of a bouquet in all public functions organized by the Government of India.

PM Modi inaugurating the programme for the 22nd Reading Day-Reading Month celebrations organized by the P.N. Panicker Foundation on 17 June 2017

Top: *Dr Manmohan Singh, former prime minister of India, inaugurating India's first Total E-Literacy Programme on 4 January 2014*

Bottom: *Pranab Mukherjee, former president of India, flagging off the outreach programme, Jan Vigyan Vikas Yatra, on 30 October 2012*

Top: *Pratibha Devisingh Patil, former president of India, inaugurating the closing ceremony of the 100th birth anniversary celebrations of P.N. Panicker on 13 August 2010*

Bottom: *M. Hamid Ansari, former vice president of India, inaugurating the Digital Library Project (conceived by the P.N. Panicker Foundation) on 30 August 2016*

Ram Nath Kovind, former president of India, unveiling the 12-foot statue of P.N. Panicker at Poojappura, Thiruvananthapuram, on 23 December 2021

N. Balagopal with President Droupadi Murmu

N. Balagopal receiving the National Award for Outstanding Efforts in Science and Technology Communication (Category-A) for the year 2021 on behalf of the P.N. Panicker Foundation

Top: *Justice (Retd.) P. Sathasivam, former governor of Kerala, inaugurating the Digital Library*

Bottom: *Chief Minister of Kerala, Pinarayi Vijayan, flagging off the P.N. Panicker Foundation's youth-focused anti-drug and anti-liquor outreach campaign on Panicker's 114th birth anniversary*

Top: *Prime Minister Narendra Modi's 'Mann ki Baat' being broadcasted in the rural areas of Kerala*

Bottom: *N. Balagopal leading an Awareness Yatra on Reading and Digital Reading as part of the Reading Month celebrations*

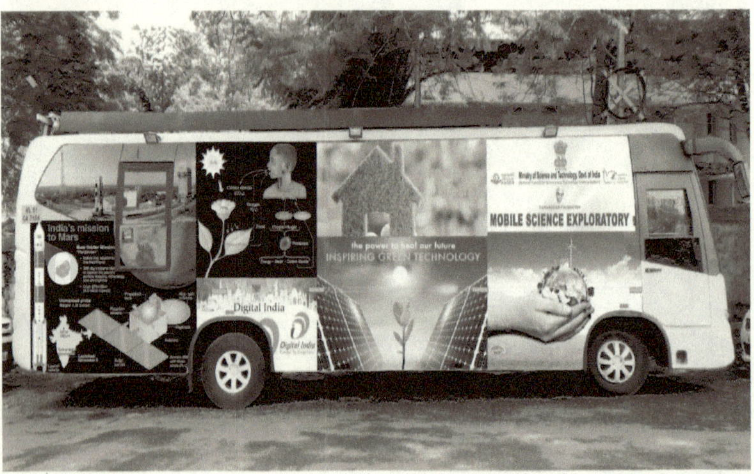

Top: *Justice (Retd.) P. Sathasivam flagging off the Digi Gaon Yatra of the unique Mobile Science Exploratory/Digital Library on 21 April 2017*

Bottom: *The Mobile Science Exploratory designed and developed by the P.N. Panicker Foundation as part of 'taking science to the masses'*

Top: *Chief Minister of Kerala, Pinarayi Vijayan, flagging off the Mobile Covid Vaccination Centre on 29 September 2021*

Bottom: *N. Balagopal educating the Centre of Indian Trade Unions' labourers on the prevention of Covid-19 and distributing masks*

Schoolchildren embracing the pledge practiced by P.N. Panicker—'Read and Grow'—during a Reading Day celebration

Top: *Conducting rural engineering demonstration classes as part of the Skill Development for Employability Enhancement programme for encouraging self-employment, wage employment and co-employment*

Bottom: *Empowering women with car servicing skills in the presence of P.K. Sreemathy (popularly known as Sreemathy Teacher)*

Top: *N. Balagopal (extreme right) with other prominent leaders at the launch of the National Digital Library of India on 19 June 2018 by the then Union Minister of Human Resource Development, Prakash Javadekar (second from left)*

Bottom: *N. Balagopal delivering the welcome address at the 24th National Reading Day-Reading Month celebrations*

Project inauguration programme of the Moringa Bio-Diversity Park in Ramanathapuram, Tamil Nadu—a joint initiative of the P.N. Panicker Foundation, NITI Aayog, Government of India and Government of Tamil Nadu

A family photo of P.N. Panicker

6

TRIUMPHS AND TEARS

Great men's later lives are often tinged with tragedy, reflecting the profound depths of their feelings. Though Socrates and Gandhi seemed to be unaffected by the external torment, they did suffer internally. In the words of the philosopher Hegel, 'Genuine tragedies in the world are not conflicts between right and wrong. They are conflicts between two rights.'

What history witnessed during Panicker's era was just some of his tragedies. Despite facing a fall from a position earned through untold sufferings and hardships, he refused to succumb to the tragedy, unlike many great men. Like a phoenix, he survived and rose above his fate, experienced resurrection and initiated a miraculous cultural episode in Kerala. One thing is absolutely certain that he was expelled from the general secretaryship of the Sangham, an organization that he laid the foundation of by offering invaluable toil and tears. What he had established was not a mere organization but a position in a splendorous saga of enlightenment where he, as a colossus, strolled astride over the narrow world, reminiscent of what William Shakespeare had stated in *Julius Caesar*.

Born at the threshold of the second millennium and departing the world towards its end, Panicker strolled astride Kerala like a colossus. However, what set him apart from a mere physical giant was not a robust physique or a dazzling appearance. Instead, it was his inexhaustible and unyielding willpower, coupled with a soul-stirring yearning for wisdom and knowledge that made him astonishing and enabled him to challenge the narrow world.

When the Grandhasala Sangham became a prestigious people's movement, organizational disputes naturally arose. From 1973 to 1977, infighting became explicit and affected, considerably, the day-to-day functions of the Sangham. It was at this juncture that differences emerged between Thayatt Sankaran and P.N. Panicker. Thayatt Sankaran was a staunch Gandhian and a literary critic who also worked as the editor of *Deshabhimani Weekly*, the cultural wing of the Communist Party of India (Marxist). (It is somewhat ambiguous to describe how a Gandhian can be the editor of a Marxist journal. The right answer is that he was not a pure Gandhian, but a Gandhian–Marxist.) Thayatt Sankaran worked for the Sangham for a comparatively short period. Even before his arrival, there were some differences of opinion between the government and the Sangham.

The initial disputes arose during the period of the first communist ministry of E.M.S. Namboodiripad, between 1957 and 1959. Being the education minister, Joseph Mundassery, a famous Malayalam literary critic, had the responsibility of handling the affairs of the libraries in the state. The Kerala Grandhasala Sangham had already established itself as a prominent cultural movement and had attracted national attention. When the first library conference was held at Nagpur, the only delegate from Kerala was P.N. Panicker. When the gradation committee was formed for the Sangham, Panicker was its chairman for a long period. Joseph Mundassery had nullified the financial powers of the gradation committee and divided its responsibility into three regions that were controlled by three social educational officers. The authority to decide matters of grants was vested in the hands of those officers, leading to a dispute between Panicker and the education minister. It is obvious that without the direct control of the general secretary of the Sangham, the gradation committee's function, which was its financial power, could not be fulfilled.

Joseph Mundassery in his book *Kozhinja Ilakal*[16] speaks about the Grandhasala Sangham and P.N. Panicker. Mundassery claims that he redressed the errors of Panicker and the gradation committee, but he never names Panicker

[16]Mundassery, Joseph, *Kozhinja Ilakal*, Current Books, Thrissur, 2004.

in the book. It is interesting to note that the head of the communist ministry of 1957, E.M.S. Namboodiripad, had no disagreement with Panicker. Though Panicker was a Gandhian in his political ideology, it was generally believed that he was held in high regards by E.M.S. Namboodiripad. Despite all disputes and disagreements that originated within the Kerala Grandhasala Sangham during this period, P.N. Panicker was acutely conscious of the need to secure unanimous opinions in the organization and foster unity and integrity in action. The systematic collation of parallel extant sources on P.N. Panicker's life fleshes out an exciting picture of colourful triumph over the challenges that he encountered surrounded by dangers and adversarial enemies.

Panicker's role in reconstructing the rural life of Kerala remains a less-explored aspect of his legacy. Recognizing the pivotal role of the young generation in this process, Panicker foresaw that literacy, including computer literacy, was indispensable for the success of this endeavor. Here, we can realize the unsurpassed far-sightedness of Panicker in discerning the imperative of literacy in the reconstruction of rural life in the country. He was infinitely passionate in his efforts towards attaining full literacy in the country. His thirst for wisdom, quest for culture and professed love for humanity made him one of the cultural architects of modern Kerala.

The Kerala Grandhasala Sangham election of 1973 was

a milestone in the library movement in Kerala, ushering in the dominance of Left politics in the library mission of the state and paving the exit for P.N. Panicker from the Sangham. This led to the origin of the KANFED movement and even after the victory of the Left, Panicker did not severe his ties with the organization.

P.N. Panicker, with the assistance of P. Govinda Pillai, N.V. Krishna Warrier and P.T. Bhaskara Panicker, launched many periodicals. He was also an author, having published nearly fifteen books, some of which are as follows:

1. *Purogathiyum Bodhavalkkaranavum*
2. *Janangalkku Padikkanam*
3. *Veetammamarkku oru Pusthakam*

Panicker was also the editor of many books published by KANFED.

Sakshara Keralam was a publication started with the joint efforts of P.T. Bhaskara Panicker, Dr N.P. Pillai, N.V. Krishna Warrier and Dr Sivadasan Pillai. P.N. Panicker initiated the publishing of nearly a hundred books for neo-literates. He also spearhead the launch of the publication series *Darsana Mala*. The credit for starting the Grandhasala manual (1948) and publishing the Grandhasala directory (1964) also goes to Panicker.

When the state literacy council was formed, P.N. Panicker was at the forefront of the movement. His attempt to improve non-formal education was a turning point in the history of Kerala. The Kerala Literary Act of 1989 was a breakthrough, democratizing the realm of libraries and serving as a global model, earning the moniker 'Kerala Model'. The foundation of the movement was, of course, laid by Panicker and we are deeply indebted to this legacy of a golden culture that is universal literacy. Without it, our assertion of democracy would have remained unfulfilled. Laila T. Abraham, deputy librarian of the university library of Mahatma Gandhi University, writes:

> The importance of non-formal education is evident from the educational experience and activities of the past decades. Rural people suffer from inadequate and weak educational facilities. They are discriminated with respect to the benefits of social and economic development due to lack of proper education. Formal education is time bound, rigid and stereotyped, which is not related to real life, giving emphasis to syllabi, textbook, timetables and examinations. Non-formal education is organized outside the infrastructure of the institution, which is learner-oriented and life-related. It is rather a supplement for formal education. The approach of non-formal education is much suitable for rural masses since it is based on their needs and environmental conditions. It reaches the deprived and disadvantaged, those who are outside the formal system of education. In the present scenario, formal

education still remains unattainable to most people in the rural areas. Non-formal education, hence, becomes the way out of the problems of illiteracy, population explosion, poverty and ignorance.

KERALA ASSOCIATION FOR NON-FORMAL EDUCATION

The principal goal of KANFED was to spread non-formal education across the state. To achieve this objective, KANFED organized several training programmes, workshops and seminars, art rallies and vehicle rallies across the state under the active leadership of P.N. Panicker. This literacy mission led by him on behalf of KANFED was a mass movement, which was, in a sense, the first people's non-formal literacy movement in the state and attracted attention at the national level, inspiring similar movements in other states.

The movement heralded by Panicker achieved great momentum and people's recognition. The Kerala Grandhasala Sangham, Kerala Sasthra Sahithya Parishad (KSSP) and other NGOs played an active role in propagating non-formal education in Kerala. KANFED's mission also covered post-literacy programmes. Several periodicals were published for neo-literates during this period. Adult education programmes introduced by

KANFED were a breakthrough in the cultural history of Kerala, cementing the secular and democratic fabric of our society.

It should be borne in mind that one of the principal associates of Panicker in the endeavour of mobilizing the mission of KANFED was Dr K. Sivadasan Pillai, the Associate Secretary General of the International Association of Educators for World Peace. Dr Sooranad Kunjan Pillai, K. Raveendran Nair, Dr K.N. Pai, Dr N.P. Pillai, Dr N.V. Krishna Warrier and B.S. Balachandran were some others who contributed significantly to this venture. The Centre for Political Research and Training (CPRT) also emerged as one of the key organizations behind the mobilization of the non-formal literacy mission in Kerala.

Public libraries should be seen as community centres rather than academic spaces, and the present centres should be able to provide sufficient accessible services for people. KANFED, CPRT, KSSP and various other NGOs and universities, along with several intellectuals, worked together in awakening Kerala to achieve full literacy and foster a culturally enriched society. During the period of the Left government in the 1980s, the Saksharatha Mission was initiated to advance literacy programmes. The mission later came to be known as the State Literacy Mission.

P.N. Panicker, under the auspices of KANFED, introduced the grand project of launching Friendly Villages

(Souhruda Gramas) throughout the state, in which disputes were to be settled without going to court. Unfortunately, he passed away before he could accomplish it. The project aimed to have one volunteer for every 10 houses and was inaugurated on 27 March 1993. The initial discussion held at the Mar Thoma Church in Thiruvalla was inaugurated by the state planning board chairman, V. Ramachandran. In his inaugural speech, V. Ramachandran emphasized the significance of Friendly Villages in the state and praised P.N. Panicker for inspiring the people, especially the new generation. At that conference, V. Ramachandran expressed his deep longing to work for the cause of Friendly Villages. K.P. Nambiar, the state planning board secretary, presided over the meeting. The keynote speech was delivered by P.N. Panicker himself and it inspired the audience to work dedicatedly for society, making them conscious of the importance of the reconstruction of the nation. He stressed the significance of literacy and non-formal education for national integrity, national unity and national reconstruction.

Justice V.R. Krishna Iyer was one of the close associates of P.N. Panicker in his social activities. As a result of Krishna Iyer's work, KANFED obtained support for the Neethi Vedi Programme from the Ford Foundation, which aimed to empower women. The full social and cultural impact of Panicker's works are yet to be comprehensively evaluated, but according to Sukumar Azhikode, when the efforts of P.N. Panicker would get realized, the university vice chancellors and the education ministers would flee the country out of shame. He writes:

> Without the background of any material possessions, he rose from the teachers' community, which was an oppressed community at that time. The society of teachers was such especially before independence. Now teachers belong to an affluent society. At that period, if a teacher had to rise from the teachers' community, he/she had to be its leader. Lacking this attribute, Panicker had the conviction that a teacher's duty is not confined to the textbooks alone. He believed that knowledge is not the legacy of one who inherits it. He was well aware that the horizon of wisdom will not end within the roof of the school.

One of the major roles of a teacher is to broaden the horizons of students, showing them the entire array of activities. In that sense, P.N. Panicker served as a noble educator of the state and a pioneering figure for the entire nation.

7

RISE OF THE PHOENIX

P.N. Panicker's humility and dedication to his work were evident in various aspects of his life. As mentioned earlier, the Government of Kerala allotted him a state car, ordered by C.H. Mohammed Koya, the then chief minister of Kerala, in 1971. This was a token of appreciation given to him for his meritorious and outstanding services in organizing libraries and literary programmes.

The state car with a number plate marked Kerala State-53 reached Panicker's rented house in Easwaravilasam Road, Trivandrum. Panicker examined the car and asked his son N. Balagopal to accompany him to Cliff House, the official residence of the chief minister. During the meeting, Panicker expressed his gratitude for the state car but requested the CM to take it back as it was a facility used exclusively by the governor and ministers of the state. He clarified that, being a dedicated social worker, he did not desire any special privileges associated with government authority. However, the CM smiled at him and stated that Panicker, in his role of serving the public for their emancipation, had the rightful claim to use such a car. The CM further instructed N. Balagopal to take his father back home in the same car. This incident vividly illustrates Panicker's modesty and reluctance to assume any special status, even when offered official perks for his selfless service. Panicker's approach to claiming his travelling allowance (TA) serves as a remarkable example for both government officials and committed social workers. As the head of the institution, he was entitled to avail TA for Class 1 officers, making him eligible to travel in first-class train compartments, use taxis and receive dearness allowance and other allowances.

Panicker never claimed TA as per the established rules and regulations. He never opted for first-class train compartments, travelling only in third-class, and attached the corresponding tickets along with the bus tickets while filling his TA. During trips to northern Kerala, he often received invitation to travel with others. If he travelled in a private car, he used to write, 'Travelled in "X" car with free fare' in the TA bill, something unseen in any of the bills submitted to the government. If he was provided free lunch and dinner and a night stay, he recorded 'free dinner' and 'free stay' in the TA bill.

His TA bills, signed by education ministers and chief ministers, became a topic of discussion among government officials in the secretariat. Seeing his TA bills, the accountant general of the state, Kuriakose, came over to the Grandhasala Sangham office and commended Panicker for his honesty in dealing with public money.

WALKING THROUGHOUT THE STATE

The People's Library Movement started by P.N. Panicker was not done upon a whim, nor was it a mere intellectual pursuit. Rather, it was the outcome of his extensive travels through thousands of villages in Kerala, where he engaged with people, particularly the youth. Known for his special fondness and connection with young individuals, Panicker tirelessly worked to establish libraries in every village across the state. However, achieving this goal was not without its challenges.

Factors like caste, religious beliefs, traditional practises, religious rituals, social inequalities, economic disparities, superstitions and male domination in society and family were obstacles to his mission of setting up libraries in villages. Moreover, most of these places were so backward that many had no facilities for proper schooling and students would drop out of school due to poverty. It was a great challenge for Panicker to overcome these obstacles but he did it with his unique willpower and industriousness. Wearing a dhoti and a khadi shirt, P.N. Panicker walked hundreds of miles daily from dawn to late night. In the midst of his ongoing mission, he did not bother about food or personal comfort. An unknown impulse inherent in him propelled him in his endeavour to make people aware of the importance of reading books to overcome grievances.

Professor S. Guptan Nair, who actively collaborated with P.N. Panicker in his library movement, details all these in his essay, 'Aparajithanaya Porali'. Guptan Nair remembers two incidents when both of them undertook a journey to Malabar. Panicker and Guptan walked and visited the village libraries throughout the day. By 8 p.m., they were totally exhausted and Guptan suggested stopping for a while to have dinner. However, Panicker was not ready to eat as he wanted to visit one more library. On another day, both of them had to spend the night on a sand mount in front of the Mattancherry railway station. Without proper food, medical treatment, sleep and rest, Panicker laboriously worked to provide an impetus to the people's library movement and the literacy movement in Kerala. It is said that he made repeated visits to numerous remote libraries across the state, covering the expanse from Kasaragod to Trivandrum.

In public life, P.N. Panicker set an unparalleled example by remaining immune to social evils like nepotism, corruption, desire for a luxuriant lifestyle, servitude and groupism. He believed that a public activist or a social worker should fulfil their duties for society consciously and conscientiously. When transport facilities were negligent, Panicker happily travelled across the whole state on foot; he never thought that he was making a sacrifice.

Panicker's mission was to liberate people from social hierarchy, slavery and ignorance. His conviction was that reading would enlighten and release them from outdated beliefs and rituals. Moreover, he believed that the nation could only be reconstructed through proper education. Recognizing the limited access to higher education in many villagers, he advocated for non-formal education for adults and initiated the library movement. The success of distance education programmes in Kerala, initiated by various universities in India, is attributed to Panicker's pioneering efforts in launching the library movement and literacy movement in the state. Many other states in our country, following the footsteps of P.N. Panicker, have been introducing these experiments in their states.

THE GLORIOUS ORGANIZER

The organizational ability of P.N. Panicker is to be specially mentioned here. Although not a professional organizer by trade, he demonstrated a natural aptitude for it. In the initial stages of his mission to launch the library movement in Kerala, there was no uniformity in the organization of house libraries. Panicker's efforts were a solo endeavour, an electrifying mission that he never abandoned as the people of the time wholeheartedly embraced his cause. He visited numerous ministers and political leaders over and over for the cause of the library, trying to get grants, inviting dignitaries to inaugurate functions, promoting libraries, facilitating the registration of journals of the libraries, etc.

Panicker wandered around the state, collecting books for the libraries. While some mocked and chided him, benevolent individuals like K.G. Parameswaran Pillai helped him out by providing a number of books. Thus, he collected thousands of books from houses across the state while approaching the different responses with extraordinary equanimity. Thaipprambil Narayanan Nair's memoirs throw light on P.N. Panicker's dedicated efforts. He recalls an occasion when he and Panicker were travelling in Thiruvalla Taluk. It was late evening and it was getting dark. Both of them were walking on a path in the midst of a field. Midway, Panicker slipped and fell in the mud. It took time to wash his clothes in a stream. In his wet clothes, he continued walking for two miles. This incident is a testament to the few hardships Panicker faced during his efforts to build the library movement in Kerala. Starvation and challenges never disoriented him but rather fuelled his determination to advance the mission. Once Panicker had gone to Ettumanoor to take part in a function regarding the rebuilding work of the library. There, he satisfied his hunger by having a banana and fresh water. He ate with a smile but the people gathered there were sad to see that sight.

One of the remarkable organizational achievements of P.N. Panicker was the unification and amalgamation of several library clusters in the state. When C. Achutha Menon became the chief minister of Kerala, he reinstated Panicker in the Kerala Library Association on 16 March 1977 when the government assumed control of libraries, overseen by the control board. The Left government had a hidden agenda of taking control of the Grandhasala Sangham, and Thayatt Sankaran, the president of the Sangham, played an important role in all these plans. He wanted to oust Panicker both from the secretaryship and the Grandhasala Sangham. According to Pattom G. Ramachandran Nair, the Malaylam biographer of P.N. Panicker, I.V. Das, the former secretary of the Library Council, had said that E.M.S. Namboodiripad had openly expressed his disgust about the steps taken by the power-hungry careerists under the leadership of Thayatt Sankaran.

Despite the support Panicker received from many veteran reformers, he grieved deeply as he witnessed heart-wrenching scenes at his office. One particularly unusual incident was when his government car granted by the then chief minister was locked in a shed. Thayatt Sankaran had seized the key to the car. This was only the beginning of the severe infighting that grew in the organization. Until then, the organization had not witnessed such political machinations and scheming.

There was vigorous competition among mainstream political parties to usurp the Grandhasala Sangham, and in this unscrupulous tussle, Panicker found himself becoming a victim. The developments in the organization in 1977 left him frustrated and upset but leaving the Sangham, as far as Panicker was concerned, was akin to leaving his mother. His relationship with the organization was not that of a mechanically nominated official but one that had been laboriously nurtured over a period of time. Grandhasala Sangham was his family; he loved all the members of the library across the state like brothers and sisters. He inspired them and persuaded them to build libraries, collect books and read. Panicker longed to mould Friendly Villages in all parts of Kerala.

His fight against illiteracy was fuelled by the conviction that reading books would awaken people and lead to social harmony, peace and togetherness. He wanted to uplift the downtrodden and oppressed people and specifically focussed on children and women. Panicker was working towards a silent revolution based on cultural integration and enlightenment.

I have already mentioned the continued work of P.N. Panicker in the remote villages throughout Kerala. His task there was not only to lay the foundation for the library movement but to create means of addressing the grievances of the people, especially the youth. Recognizing the plight of educated yet unemployed youth, Panicker collaborated with the Khadi Commission and Khadi Board. With the help of A.M. Thomas, the then chairman of the Khadi Commission, Panicker founded KEDES. Justice V.R. Krishna Iyer was the chairman of KEDES and A.M. Thomas was the vice chairman. These aspects of Panicker's organizational and humanitarian efforts have unfortunately been overlooked by cultural historians in Kerala.

There may have been library movements in other states of India but nowhere will we see a movement that had the ground support of the masses like Panicker's library movement. The achievements of this movement were the direct outcomes of Panicker's unwavering dedication and tireless efforts, symbolized by the blood and sweat he invested in its cause. He wanted to establish a national-level library movement, demonstrating a broad national perspective in building the People's Library Movement.

Unlike many other states where libraries are often reserved for academic students and researchers, Kerala opened the doors of its libraries for all. Panicker firmly believed that libraries should belong to the general people and have the wholehearted support of the masses. He enlisted volunteers for social activities and inculcated in them the fundamental lessons of leadership based on honesty, commitment and service.

Panicker also took steps to emancipate people who struggled with addiction. He participated in and was actively involved in the work of many organizations like the Sahithya Pravarthaka Sangham, Samastha Kerala Sahithya Parishad, Children's Film Society, State Temple Proclamation Committee, Kerala Tourism Development Committee and the State Scheduled Caste/Scheduled Tribes (SC/ST) Committee. He was also the executive director of the State Resource Centre.

Kerala's government began celebrating 19 June as Vayanadinam (Reading Day) with a week-long series of cultural activities and programmes in schools and colleges to promote reading habits among students and teachers. These celebrations in schools, colleges and other public institutions took place to honour the great contributions of P.N. Panicker, the father of the library movement in Kerala. The chief minister of Kerala, Pinarayi Vijayan, inaugurating one of the statewide Reading Week (Vayana varam) celebrations in schools organized in memory of Panicker, said:

> Libraries in our state play a vital role in shaping our culture in addition to improving reading skills. Libraries in our villages have played a major role in spreading the messages of the state's renaissance movements among the public.

Addressing the students and teachers at Government Model Girls' Higher Secondary School, Pattom, he said[17]:

---

[17]*Times of India*, 21 June 2019.

> The mottos put forward by the library movement had created a great change in society. When it comes to it, we can't forget P.N. Panicker and his co-worker, I.V. Das, for their immense contributions to the library movement. Students should always remember that Narayana Guru and Kunjunni Mash had spoken about the power of reading and the need to cultivate the habit among youngsters. All students should make reading a habit and must find time to maintain that habit.

The library movement that was founded by P.N. Panicker resulted in a vast proportion of the population of the state making a habit of reading books and libraries became cultural centres where people, especially youngsters, engaged in group discussions and debates on burning issues, of both national and international relevance.

Panicker dedicated his life to the library movement. The conspicuous skill explicit in the personality of Panicker was that he was able to solve any problem that originated in the Grandhasala Sangham. In 1977, the state government took control of the Sangham through an ordinance, causing widespread discontent. The Grandhasala Sangham was always a people's democratic body, an independent and autonomous cultural centre where people came together to read and interact. In that sense, it was a community centre. Reading books was not the only duty of the members of the library; they also discharged other imperative sociocultural tasks. However, the developments of 1977 had dispirited Panicker. An anguished Panicker, fed up with the infighting within the organization, stepped down from the Grandhasala Sangham but continued his mission through KANFED, a civil society organization promoting adult education.

The organizational issues of Grandhasala Sangham became a controversial subject during that period and any chance of a quick turnaround was impossible. State hegemony over the Sangham overshadowed the decentralization of power. There is a misguided notion that to sustain an organization, it is best to bring it under state control. However, this is more in line with state capitalism than socialism. Public property or institutions should be democratically controlled by elected members of the public and not by officials selected by the government or its nominated agents as gradual state control eventually leads to totalitarianism.

When a control body was placed above the elected body of the Grandhasala Sangham in 1977, the Kerala government basically terminated the democratization of thousands of libraries in Kerala. Once blissful houses of reading, togetherness, interaction and open discussions, these libraries became 'quiet' jails. The librarians with their new-found authority were not aware of the basic goal of a library, instead emphasizing 'silence and discipline' as the mottos of reading. They ignored the social goal of the library. Reading is a means, not the end; it should inevitably lead to innovative thinking, imagination, furthering of studies and, above all, encompassing social and cultural activities.

Leaving the Grandhasala Sangham was a sad moment for Panicker. He was already debarred from the control body of the organization; Panicker's expulsion could be seen as a metaphorical patricide of democracy. Despite the hardships and heartbreaks, Panicker's resilience and fortitude empowered him to rise again like a phoenix.

Panicker received appeals from the ruling elite, including IAS officers, urging him to reconstitute the library council as a trust to secure a lifelong position as general secretary; Panicker steadfastly rejected these requests. Instead, he passionately advocated for the restoration of democratic processes in the libraries.

DEATH AND AFTER

On 19 June 1995, P.N. Panicker, the towering figure of the library and literacy movement, passed away at the Government Medical College, Trivandrum, due to severe myocardial infarction, at the age of 86. He remained active in outreach awareness programmes to educate the common man on the need for reading and literacy till he breathed his last.

P.N. Panicker was the first social development activist of the state to be honoured with a state funeral that included a police band and gun salute. His body lay in state at the government auditorium—the VJT Hall, Trivandrum. All state ministers, including the chief minister, government officials and the general public came in thousands to pay their last respects to the departed 'Akshara Guru' and offered floral tributes. The masses organized a padayatra that accompanied his body, in a decorated government vehicle, to the funeral ground 3 km away.

On the 41st day of his demise, his mortal remains were collected in 16 urns, wrapped in holy cloth and transported in a special coach of the Parasuram Express from Trivandrum to Mangalore, touching all the 14 districts of Kerala. This was facilitated by Southern Railway as a tribute to Panicker. The Government of Kerala instructed all 14 district collectors to receive the urns containing P.N. Panicker's ashes from N. Balagopal, his eldest son, at the respective railway stations where the Parasuram Express made stops. They were to organize a padayatra to immerse the sacred ashes in the holy river of the district. This was a practice usually reserved for leaders such as Mahatma Gandhi, Jawaharlal Nehru and Indira Gandhi, whose ashes were traditionally immersed in three or four holy rivers of the state with government involvement.

As a mark of respect to Panicker, a great personality who dedicated his whole life to establishing libraries in all villages and achieving 100 per cent literacy in the state, the Government of Kerala declared his first annual remembrance day to be observed as 'Reading Day'. Initiated in 1996, the day-long celebrations of Reading Day evolved into Reading Week, Reading Fortnight celebration and from 2017, Reading Month. These celebrations encompass activities in all schools, colleges, panchayats, etc., of the country as per the direction of Shri Narendra Modi, the Hon'ble Prime Minister of India. What originated in Kerala as a regional observance has now expanded to encompass all 28 states and 9 union territories of India as well as 9 foreign countries, touching a population of 3.15 million.

On 19 June 2018, the Government of India dedicated the prestigious Digital Library project, funded at ₹1,600 crore, to the nation in honour of P.N. Panicker, who was instrumental in introducing inclusive education with his simple slogan 'Vayichu Valaruka' (Read and Grow) that he preached and practised throughout his lifetime. The programme was organized at a colourful event held at Vigyan Bhavan, New Delhi, with a host of Union ministers and officials.

During the eighth anniversary of Reading Day on 19 June 2003, the Government of Kerala and the P.N. Panicker Foundation together, for the first time in the country, initiated Digital Reading using internet-enabled services.

The Government of Kerala erected a 12-foot bronze statue of P.N. Panicker at Poojappura, near the Maha Sree

Saraswathi Temple where the Vidyarambham[18] ritual has been performed for decades. The statue was unveiled by the then President of India, Ram Nath Kovind, in the esteemed presence of the state governor, chief minister and other high officials of the state.

In June 2004, the postal department honoured P.N. Panicker through the issuance of a commemorative postage stamp.

[18]Vidyarambham signifies the formal introduction of toddlers to the world of writing and learning. 'Vidya' means knowledge and 'arambham' means start, making it a ceremony that marks the beginning of a child's educational journey. During this ritual, children are initiated into the process of reading and writing, typically by tracing letters in a tray of rice or on a slate, with the help of a learned person.

8

THE LEGACY

The P.N. Panicker Foundation was launched on his 84th birth anniversary (Sathabhishekam) by B. Rachaiah, the then governor of Kerala, in the august presence of K. Karunakaran, chief minister of Kerala.

The P.N. Panicker Foundation was chaired by Justice V.R. Krishna Iyer and he held the post till he breathed his last. The Foundation's primary objective was to promote reading habits among children and rural populations and develop a culture of appreciating books.

One of the Foundation's prestigious initiatives, Digital Library and Digital Literacy, was widely appreciated and officially recognized by both the state and central governments. The mission is all-encompassing, envisioning e-literacy and the enhancement of e-libraries for the people of India. It aims at familiarizing the masses with the use of ICT in acquiring knowledge and skills for enhancing their living standards and for greater creativity via the internet. The Foundation proposes the use of e-literacy for the public and for neo-literates to enable their skill development. Providing special services to the disadvantaged classes is also one of the major aims of the Foundation.

N. Balagopal, a key figure in the P.N. Panicker Foundation, has dedicated his life to the fulfilment of the above-mentioned goals. He has stamped his authority in the informal and digital literacy domains. Following in the footsteps of his distinguished father, P.N. Panicker, N. Balagopal stands as a symbolic figure with extensive experience and an innovative spirit, who has succeeded in popularizing digital library and digital literacy to a considerable extent. Like his father, N. Balagopal is proficient in interacting with a diverse range of individuals, including prime ministers, presidents, litterateurs and other influential figures in society. His ability to attract and influence people from all walks of life is exceptional, catapulting the P.N. Panicker Foundation to national prominence.

DIGITAL LITERACY

Digital literacy refers to an individual's ability to find, evaluate and generate clear information through writing and other media across various digital platforms. It works on the conviction that people should have easy access to educational and employment opportunities. The P.N. Panicker Foundation focusses on removing barriers that obstruct the youth from exploring digital opportunities.

Digital literacy aims at streamlining and enhancing student learning; supporting collaboration, interaction, broad communication and creativity; and equipping students with the skills and expertise that they require to work and live in a globalized world. The P.N. Panicker Foundation actively responds to the pressing need to enhance digital competency among people. Ultimately, the project aspires to empower all citizens, with substantial support from tutors, trainers and policymakers, ensuring their proficiency in the digital landscape.

ONE LIBRARY ALL OF INDIA

'One Library All of India' is the watchword of the innovative mission heralded by the P.N. Panicker Foundation under the leadership of N. Balagopal, which has ushered a brilliant era in the digital education history of India. His pioneering work[19] has garnered praise from Indian Prime Ministers Dr Manmohan Singh and Narendra Modi, Indian Presidents Pratibha Devisingh Patil and Pranab Mukherjee, and Vice President M. Hamid Ansari for its epoch-making impact.

The Ministry of Human Resource Development dedicated this endeavour to the nation on Reading Day

[19]The P.N. Panicker Foundation website (https://www.pnpanickerfoundation.org/) serves as a platform to facilitate and disseminate information about these missions.

on 19 June 2018 to commemorate the annual remembrance day of P.N. Panicker.

ONE KNOWLEDGE HUB

The digital library and digital literacy missions were significant leaps forward in the cultural history of Kerala that facilitated the attempts of the public, especially youngsters, to sow the seeds of digital ambitions and also to be part of the national reconstruction and national integration.

There are several realms of life in which the P.N. Panicker Foundation has its stake. They are as follows:

1. Animal husbandry
2. Drying and fisheries
3. Biotechnology and culture
4. Children, civic issues
5. Differently-abled
6. Disaster management
7. Dalit upliftment
8. Drinking water
9. Education and literacy
10. Environment and forests
11. Food processing
12. Health and family welfare
13. HIV/AIDS

14. Housing, human rights
15. Information and communication technology
16. Legal awareness, labour and employment
17. Land resources
18. Microfinance
19. Minority issues
20. Micro, small and medium enterprises

P.N. PANICKER VIGYAN VIKAS KENDRA

P.N. Panicker Vigyan Vikas Kendra has been constituted by the Government of Kerala as an autonomous body to promote reading and digital reading and the development of scientific temper under the chairmanship of the education minister of the state.

The P.N. Panicker Vigyan Vikas Kendra is an attempt at reconstructing Kerala as the first e-literate state of the country. With the assistance of the National e-Governance Plan, ICT is being taken to remote corners of the nation, giving access to the rural masses so that they reap the benefit of the development of IT. Some of the projects that the Foundation undertook are IT mass literacy, programmes for women/SC/ST candidates, the National Digital Literacy Mission, total digital literacy through e-literacy, etc.

N. Balagopal, the vice chairman of the P.N. Panicker Foundation, is at the forefront and committed to excellence. In 2002, the organization initiated the popularizing of e-reading among the masses with internet facilities. His endeavour led to the establishment of more than 25,000 rural home e-libraries in 2010. As an extension of its broad prospects, the Foundation proposes to collaborate with the state central library at Trivandrum and three district libraries-cum-knowledge centres in selected panchayats to provide digital libraries for people from all walks of life.

Digital libraries are established to eliminate the existing barriers posed by traditional libraries and equip learners with up-to-date knowledge comprehensively and quickly. They provide services like references, which are a blessing to knowledge-loving learners regardless of their age, gender and academic standards. The national digital library emphasizes non-formal education, which will benefit 60 per cent of the Indian population. It is committed to advancing the digital library, which will bring about inclusive education as well as universalization of education. The national digital library is the fulfilment of our national poet Rabindranath Tagore's lifelong fascination and dream for a splendorous and free nation with an ever-widening knowledge domain.

P.N. Panicker launched the people's library movement with the mission of 'Education for All', which heralded Kerala's development, later widely acclaimed as the 'Kerala Model'. The model has been recognized as an illustrious example and concept, inspiring the global community. Now N. Balagopal is carrying forward the legacy by spearheading efforts to popularize the digital library movement. As the torchbearer of the mission, he exhibits resilience, diligence, a spirit of accommodation and, above all, magnanimity, excelling in the national tasks at hand.

APPENDIX

SPEECH BY THE FORMER PRESIDENT OF INDIA, PRATIBHA DEVISINGH PATIL

Ladies and Gentlemen,

I am happy to participate in the Closing Ceremony of the Centenary Celebrations of the father of the Library and Literacy Movement of Kerala, Shri P.N. Panicker. Literacy culture has become a part of the ethos of Kerala with education receiving encouragement. In this, the contribution of Shri P.N. Panicker has been immeasurable. His vision, his identification with the common people and his commitment to improve their lives has made him a legendary figure worth emulating.

Considered as one of the principal architects of modern Kerala, Shri Panicker lived a life devoted to the cause of literacy and to the development of the State. Shri Panicker was deeply interested in educating agricultural workers, encouraging them to study, which is all the more necessary these days. His area of work gradually expanded. With his 'Read and Grow' slogan, the library and literacy movement started by him spread to every nook and corner of Kerala. So good was his work through the Aksharakeralam project that Kerala became the first fully literate state in the country. The project and its approach provided valuable inputs and lessons for the National Literacy Mission. Shri Panicker's name, thus, is linked to the cause of literacy not only in Kerala but also at the national level.

Shri P.N. Panicker was also the driving spirit behind the concept of Kerala Grandhasala Sangham set up in 1945 with 47 rural libraries. It was designed for adult and non-formal education activities to be undertaken in an organized manner in Kerala, with 6,000 libraries drawn into this network. Shri Panicker spearheaded the setting up of these libraries and reading rooms as community centres for social activities through useful discussions, seminars and symposia on social and developmental issues. In this way, libraries fulfilled their role as social institutions capable of shaping attitudes and values of people. [...]

There is also need for modernizing libraries and building global access. Libraries now have the possibility of developing extensive external networks by using technologies. They can develop partnerships with other libraries, educational institutions and research centres. The exchange of information between libraries would help in adopting better practices for libraries, such as cataloging and preservation of records. They can also share with each other perspectives on how to deal with new concepts like e-libraries and digital libraries, which provide a platform for giving access to libraries. Who can access, how and on what terms are some of the issues that can be discussed between the libraries of the world. In this context, it is of interest that the P.N. Panicker Foundation has in recent times been harnessing technology in its attempt to popularize e-reading, through making available computers to rural households and connecting them with the internet. This initiative, I understand, has paved the way for the establishment of 25,000 rural home e-libraries.

The Government of Kerala every year observes June 19th, the day Shri Panicker passed away, as Vayanadinam—the Day of Reading. Inculcating the habit of reading in our children and youth is very important. Besides being a source of knowledge, reading develops their mental ability and improves concentration levels. This is especially important in our times, as children have many other sources of entertainment that provide instant gratification, such as the television, the internet, electronic games and social networking sites. The challenge is to make our children read more and attract them to read books that tell them about our heritage and cultural values.

Apart from the literacy and education work, Shri P.N. Panicker was deeply concerned with the development of Kerala, in particular the rural areas. He spent a considerable amount of time in travelling to distant parts of the State and meeting tribal people in backward areas to understand their problems and help them find solutions. He would impress upon them to give up habits like tobacco and drinking liquor, which affected their health, causing difficulties for their families and disturbing social peace. It is important that this work of Shri Panicker continues.

Shri Panicker was also a man who was a firm believer in Gandhiji's concept of living a simple life. Usually clad in Khadi, a frail figure, he was warmly welcomed wherever he travelled in Kerala. Individuals like Shri Panicker have taught us that a life of values, commitment to a cause and selfless service can bring many positive changes in society. It is, therefore, important that we keep their memories alive, and teach their ideas and vision to succeeding generations, so that they are inspired to work for the welfare of others. I am, therefore, glad that in Kerala, activities are organized at schools and public institutions to honour the contributions of Shri P.N. Panicker to the cause of development, literacy, education and the library movement.

I would also encourage the Panicker Foundation to continue to carry on his legacy. I am aware that it is undertaking a large number of socio-economic activities. I am informed that one of the activities relates to establishing litigation-free Panchayat communities, so as to create social harmony among people. Such activities that promote a peaceful and harmonious environment are essential for our society and the nation. I am also sure that the efforts of the P.N. Panicker Foundation in the myriad areas that it is working with amongst the people of this State will bear even greater fruits in the future. With these words I convey my good wishes to all present here and inaugurate the Closing Ceremony of the Centenary Celebrations of Shri P.N. Panicker.

Thank you.
Jai Hind!

(Excerpt from Pratibha Devisingh Patil's speech during the inauguration of the closing ceremony of P.N. Panicker's centenary celebrations in Thiruvananthapuram, Kerala, on 13 August 2010.)

SPEECH BY THE FORMER PRESIDENT OF INDIA, PRANAB MUKHERJEE

It gives me great pleasure to join you today to flag off the 9th Jan Vigyan Vikas Yatra. I was very much interested when I heard about this annual event organized by the P. N. Panicker Vigyan Vikas Kendra in collaboration with the Government of Kerala and other agencies. I understand that the Yatra is one of the flagship events of the Kendra—whose mission it is to spread education to reduce poverty.

I understood this to be a remarkably effective method of outreach which has proven to be successful and result oriented. It has become widely known as a focussed grassroots level campaign to encourage reading and love for books among the young. I was struck by its simplicity—and its evolution from a small reading room in a village into a movement for mass literacy—which shows that it has been embraced by the people for whom it is meant. They have not only responded, but taken full advantage of it.

It is hardly any surprise that this programme of mass contact has successfully instilled in the young people in Kerala a thirst for learning and a scientific temper by taking knowledge and the instruments of learning to those who have no access to them.

Today, the Government of India's national literacy mission draws inspiration from the work and methods of Shri P.N. Panicker.

This is also an opportunity to pay tribute to Shri P.N. Panicker, father of the library movement, who dedicated his life to initiate and guide this highly successful literacy movement.

From the Travancore Library Association that he founded in 1945 with 47 rural libraries, he developed a series of similar units, which has now grown into a network of 6,000 libraries and a tremendously successful movement for total literacy in Kerala. The results speak for themselves. Kerala has the distinction of being the first State in India to attain 100 per cent literacy.

Shri P.N. Panicker had a simple but powerful slogan, 'vayichu valaruka', which encouraged all children to read and grow.

Shri P.N. Panicker, like many of us, was driven by Gandhiji's words—that 'Mass illiteracy is India's sin and shame and must be liquidated'.

In keeping with his commitment to Gandhian ideals, he also built into his programme a campaign to foster social amity and harmony. [...]

I would like to congratulate the Government of Kerala for their observance of 19th June, the date of the passing of this great visionary, Shri P.N. Panicker, as the 'Day of Reading' which is annually marked by a week of public events and activities in schools and educational institutions. There could be no better way to honour the monumental contribution of Shri P.N. Panicker to literacy and education in this 'God's Own Country'.

With these few words, I extend my best wishes to the participants in the Jan Vigyan Vikas Yatra and wish them every success in their project.

(Excerpt from Pranab Mukherjee's speech on the occasion of flagging off the 9th Jan Vigyan Vikas Yatra organized by P.N. Panicker Vigyan Vikas Kendra in Thiruvananthapuram, Kerala, on 30 October 2012.)

SPEECH BY THE FORMER PRESIDENT OF INDIA, RAM NATH KOVIND

My dear brothers and sisters of God's own country.

Every visit to Kerala fills me with special joy.

Ladies and gentlemen,

I feel a great deal of satisfaction after unveiling the statue of the pioneer of learning, literacy and library movements, the Late P.N. Panicker. I am thankful to the members of P.N. Panicker Foundation for giving me this opportunity to be here with you all. The contributions of Shri Panicker have been so noteworthy and widely praised that leaders from different political parties have been brought together today on this stage in his memory.

This special occasion makes me think about the simple yet great vision of Shri Panicker. A visionary can see what others don't see. I believe that Shri Panicker would have seen his pioneering steps leading to the great strides Kerala took in the areas of literacy and education. An area of illiteracy can remain an area of darkness. The light of literacy can brighten the path to individual and collective progress.

I am told that the young P.N. Panicker used to read the daily newspapers to groups of illiterate people of different ages. He started a reading centre in a small room provided by the local cooperative society in his village in Kuttanad. Shri Panicker held Mahatma Gandhi in very high esteem. He wanted to remove the evil of illiteracy which Gandhiji had described as a curse and shame of the country. Shri Panicker spread a very simple and most potent message—'Vayichu Valaruka' which means 'Read and Grow'.

Shri Panicker made libraries and literacy a movement of the people. In fact, he made it a popular cultural movement. It is a unique feature of Kerala that in every village, even in the remotest villages, there is a library. People feel an emotional connect with the library in their village or town just as they feel a special connect with the temple or church or mosque or school in their village or town. Libraries created by the movement of Shri Panicker later became nerve centres of all social and cultural activities of which the literacy movement of Kerala is an impressive example. Children come to read in the libraries. Older people also come to read and meet and discuss issues relevant to them. The credit for libraries having a central place in the culture of Kerala goes to Shri P.N. Panicker who connected common people to libraries. It is understandable that when books are made easily available to the people, those who cannot read will find a trigger as well as a facility to read. The Granthashala Sangam started by Shri Panicker with about 50 small libraries in 1945 grew into a large network of thousands of libraries. Through this large network of libraries, the common people of Kerala could get to know the thoughts and ideals of Shri Narayana Guru, Ayyankali, V.T. Bhattathiripad and other great masters. The cosmopolitan outlook of an average person from Kerala can be traced to the library and literacy movement of Shri Panicker.

Ladies and gentlemen,

I am very happy to note that P.N. Panicker Foundation is carrying forward his mission with dedication. The Foundation is promoting the cause of digital literacy as a tool to realize the cause of inclusive growth. [...] I am happy to note that the Foundation started digital learning in rural areas since the beginning of this century and this effort has succeeded in establishing thousands of home digital libraries. This effort of the Foundation is a very meaningful tribute to the memory of Shri Panicker.

I must appreciate the efforts of Professor P. J. Kurien, Former Deputy Chairman, Rajya Sabha and Shri N. Balagopal, Vice Chairman of P.N. Panicker Foundation in reaching the unreached through initiatives like P.N. Panicker National Reading Mission. I have been informed that the Prime Minister Shri Narendra Modi has directed the Foundation to reach 30 crore underprivileged people in the country through the National Reading Mission by 2022. I have been told that the Foundation has made substantial progress in the direction of realizing this target.

I am happy to note that the commendable work done by the P.N. Panicker Foundation resulted in the setting up of the P.N. Panicker Vigyan Vikas Kendra by the Government of Kerala as an autonomous organization. As mandated by our Constitution, it is one of the Fundamental Duties of every citizen of India to develop the scientific temper, humanism and the spirit of inquiry and reform. The objective of the Vikas Kendra is to reduce poverty through knowledge. The Vigyan Vikas Kendra also seeks to inculcate scientific temper among the youth.

Observing the punyatithi of Shri Panicker on 19th June as 'Reading Day' is the most appropriate way of paying tribute to the great nation builder. [...]

The 'Sakshara Keralam' movement became popular and effective due to the foundations laid down by Shri Panicker. Kerala became the first State to have 100 per cent literacy. The high literacy and education levels in Kerala have had a multiplier effect. Kerala leads other states on several indices of human development, including aspects of sustainable development. Successive governments in Kerala have kept sustained focus on the agenda of growth and development. Therefore, the State has maintained its leadership position on several markers of excellence. [...]

There is a saying in Sanskrit—'Amritam tu Vidya', which means education or learning is like nectar. I once again commend the Panicker Foundation for distributing this nectar of learning in the entire country.

I extend my heartiest greetings to all of you for Christmas and wish you all a very Happy New Year.

Thank you.
Jai Hind!

(Excerpt from Ram Nath Kovind's speech on the occasion of the unveiling of the statue of P.N. Panicker in Thiruvananthapuram, Kerala, on 23 December 2021.)

SPEECH BY THE FORMER VICE PRESIDENT OF INDIA, M. HAMID ANSARI

[...] But above all, e-literacy skills and access to internet provide the citizen with an almost unlimited amount of knowledge and information. This information is the key to empowering the citizen and for the making of a successful democracy. It is therefore befitting that a network of library should be the hub of the efforts to bring about total e-literacy in the state.

I commend the government of Kerala for setting up this institution in the memory of Shri P.N. Panicker, who has left an indelible mark in the state and the rest of the country by his contributions to furthering the cause of literacy.

I also appreciate that the P.N. Panicker Vigyan Vikas Kendra has taken the lead towards realizing the aim of making Kerala the first e-literate state of the country, within a timeframe of 33 months, in collaboration with various organizations from state and the central government, and with active participation of the civil society. I have been informed that the first phase of the e-literacy programme has proceeded as per the schedule and that e-literacy has been achieved in 19 Panchayats, covering some 3.25 lakh people by March 2016.

I am very happy, therefore, to formally launch the second phase of the total e-literacy programme in Kerala today. I am informed that the second stage of total e-literacy programme would involve establishing 100 digital libraries, which will provide resources and information to over 50 lakh villagers in the state.

Kerala has been a pioneer state in terms of ushering in programmes aimed at improving the human condition and empowering the citizens. The quest for 100 per cent e-literacy is reflective of that drive and spirit. It is an outstanding attempt at empowering the citizens and providing them with e-literacy skills that will make it possible for them to participate productively in the global society and the information age.

I wish the project and those associated with it all the very best for the future.

Jai Hind!

(Excerpt from M. Hamid Ansari's speech at the inauguration of the 2nd phase of the Total e-Literacy programme at Kanakakkunnu Palace, Thiruvananthapuram, Kerala, on 30 August 2016.)

SPEECH BY THE FORMER PRIME MINISTER OF INDIA, DR MANMOHAN SINGH

I am delighted to be in Kerala once again. Let me begin by wishing all of you and the people of Kerala happiness, prosperity and success in the New Year.

We all know that Kerala is the leading State in the country in terms of indices of human development. Literacy is one of these indices and the fact that Kerala took an early lead in literacy has in turn helped it do well in the other dimensions of human development. The success of the literacy movement in Kerala owes much to a great son of the State, Shri P.N. Panicker. I join all of you in paying tribute to him as we launch this E-Literacy Project to be implemented by the P.N. Panicker Vigyan Vikas Kendra. I also compliment the Kendra for this initiative.

In today's world of instant communication and the internet, it is not easy to imagine and appreciate the difficulties which a frail man must have faced as he lit the spark of literacy in a small village in North Kerala in the first half of the last century and then spread his message to the whole of the State. Later, Shri Panicker's initiative, the Grandhasala Sangam ignited a popular cultural movement in Kerala at the end of which the State acquired total literacy in the 1990s.

The Grandhasala Sangam began humbly with 47 libraries in 1945 and grew into a network of more than 6,000 libraries spreading across the towns and villages of Kerala. Shri Panicker also established the Kerala Association for Non Formal Education and Development (KANFED). The activities of these two organizations working together made a profound impact on the education, culture and development of Kerala.

Shri Panicker also worked to foster social amity and harmony, devoting his last years to the Friendship Village Movement. He continued travelling and working vigorously, sustained by his simple Gandhian lifestyle and an indomitable will, till he passed away on 19 June 1995.

I am happy that the Government of Kerala observes 19th June annually as Vayanadinam or the Day of Reading with a week-long series of activities at schools and public institutions.

Shri Panicker left an indelible mark at the national level also. The National Literacy Mission has been inspired largely by his work.

I commend the Government of Kerala for setting up an institution to perpetuate the memory of Shri P.N. Panicker.

I am very happy that the P.N. Panicker Vigyan Vikas Kendra is taking the lead to make Kerala the first e-literate state of the country in collaboration with the central and state governments and civil society organizations.

The total e-literacy campaign to be implemented using the tools of Information and Communications Technology (ICT) will help in reducing the digital divide. This will contribute to improvements in the living standards of the underprivileged population of the state.

I am told that the P.N. Panicker Foundation, the mother organization of the P.N. Panicker Vigyan Vikas Kendra, was the first organization in the country to popularize e-reading among the rural masses. I am happy that the Vigyan Vikas Kendra is taking this work forward.

In fact we need such initiatives to be taken across the length and breadth of the country. This will help us in realizing the full potential of ICT—in decentralized governance, in better delivery of services, particularly education, in financial inclusion and in e-commerce.

The e-literacy programme will also help the common man of Kerala to participate in the exchange of ideas and information that social media enables. It will help the youth to be better equipped for making use of productive employment opportunities. It will also help in building social capital by enabling success stories of community efforts to be shared easily.

Many social historians consider the library movement

to be the cornerstone of the so-called Kerala model of development. I wish that similarly the E-Literacy Project of the Panicker Vigyan Vikas Kendra will contribute substantially to quickening the pace of Kerala's social and economic development and to political empowerment of its people. Its success will be our tribute to the great Shri P.N. Panicker. I extend my best wishes for effective implementation of the project.

Thank you.
Jai Hind!

(Dr Manmohan Singh's speech at the launch of the e-literacy programme implemented by the P.N. Panicker Vigyan Vikas Kendra on 4 January 2014 in Thiruvananthapuram, Kerala.)

SPEECH BY THE PRIME MINISTER OF INDIA, NARENDRA MODI

It gives me great pleasure to be here on the occasion of the inauguration of reading month celebration. I thank and congratulate the P.N. Panicker Foundation for organizing this. There can be no joy greater than reading and no strength greater than knowledge.

Friends,

Kerala has been a torch-bearer and inspiration to the whole nation in the field of literacy.

The first 100 per cent literate city and first 100 per cent literate district have been from Kerala. Kerala was also the first state to attain 100 per cent primary education. Some of the oldest colleges, schools and libraries of the country are also situated in Kerala.

This could not have been achieved by the Government alone. Citizens and social organizations have played an active role in this remarkable achievement. Kerala has set an example in people's participation in this regard. I admire the work of people like late Shri P.N. Panicker and his foundation. Shri P.N. Panicker was also the driving spirit behind the library network in Kerala. He did this through Kerala Grandhasala Sangham set up by him in 1945 with 47 rural libraries.

I believe that reading and knowledge should not be limited only to work-related aspects. It should help develop habits of social responsibility, service to the nation and service to humanity. It should cure the evils in society and nation. It should spread the idea of peace along with respect for unity and integrity of the nation.

It is said that one literate woman can educate two families. Kerala has set an example worthy of emulation in this regard.

I learn that the P.N. Panicker Foundation, together with a number of government agencies, private-sector entities and civil society organizations, is leading an initiative of reading.

Their target is to reach 300 million underprivileged people by 2022. The main objective of this mission is to promote reading as a means to grow and prosper.

Reading can help broaden one's thinking. A well-read population will help India excel globally. [...]

I am told that as a pilot project of Digital Libraries, the Panicker Foundation is working with 18 public libraries in the state in collaboration with Indian Public Library Movement, New Delhi.

I would like to see such a reading and library movement in the entire country. The movement should not be limited to make people literate. It should try to achieve the real goal of bringing social and economic change. The foundation of good knowledge should be followed by a superstructure of a better society.

I am happy to note that the State Government has announced 19th June as the reading day. Obviously, a lot of effort will converge to make this a popular activity.

The Government of India has also provided support to the activities of the Foundation. I am told that about 1.20 crore rupees have been given to the Foundation in the last two years.

I am also happy to see that the Foundation is now focussing on digital literacy. This is the need of the hour.

Friends!

I believe in people's power. It has the capacity to make a better society and nation.

I urge every young person in the audience to take a pledge of reading. And enable everyone to do so.

Together, we can once again make India a land of wisdom and knowledge.

Thank you.

(Excerpt from Narendra Modi's speech at the launch of P.N. Panicker Reading Day-Reading Month celebrations on 17 June 2017 in Kochi, Kerala.)

NOTE FROM THE P.N. PANICKER FOUNDATION

Shri P.N. Panicker harboured a dream of establishing a library in every village of Kerala, envisioning easy access to knowledge for his fellow citizens, especially the poorest of the poor, thus empowering them. Through tireless efforts, he established more than 5,000 libraries by travelling through the length and breadth of Kerala, touching the remotest corners and neglected tribal pockets.

To facilitate the education of the uneducated, underprivileged and school dropouts, he initiated the Literacy Movement through which Kerala achieved total literacy in 1991. His life, dedicated to this cause, was a testament to resilience marked by hardships.

Traversing the state, Panicker engaged with men and women, generating awareness and fostering a vision for Kerala to become the first totally literate state in the country. The idea, inspiration and leadership for this transformation emanated from Panicker and his organization, KANFED. This vision materialized through the statewide movement, Sakshara Keralam, a time-bound intensive campaign involving thousands of voluntary workers that succeeded on 18 April 1991.

Continuing to travel and work vigorously, sustained by his simple Gandhian lifestyle and indomitable will, Panicker dedicated himself to the cause until he passed away on 19 June 1995. Annually, on this date, the Government of Kerala observes Vayanadinam (Day of Reading) as a tribute to Panicker's significant contributions to literacy and education. The commemoration includes a week-long series of activities in schools and public institutions.

The impact of Panicker's work through the Literacy Movement extends beyond his lifetime. This frail man transformed a simple slogan of 'Read and Grow' into a powerful movement that has inspired nationwide efforts to promote literacy and education.

We are indebted to Shri P.P Sathyan, the author of this biography, and the team at Rupa Publications, New Delhi, for their exceptional support and collaboration in the publication of this volume. Additionally, we express sincere thanks and gratitude to the common men who embody the principles and perseverance championed by P.N. Panicker in the creation of knowledge-based societies.

—N. Balagopal
Vice Chairman
P.N. Panicker Foundation

ABOUT P.N. PANICKER FOUNDATION

The P.N. Panicker Foundation was established in 1993 under the chairmanship of Justice V.R. Krishna Iyer and inaugurated by Shri B. Rachaiah, the Governor of Kerala, in the presence of Shri K. Karunakaran, the then Chief Minister of Kerala and T.M. Jacob, the then Minister for Education, Government of Kerala. Inaugurated during the Sathabhishekam Celebrations (84th birth anniversary) of P.N. Panicker, the Foundation strives to carry forward his legacy by inculcating reading habit among children, promoting school reading clubs, practicing Gandhian Philosophy of 'earning while learning', imparting total digital literacy, equipping youth with skill development for employability enhancement, focussing on effective science communication, developing rural entrepreneurship, popularizing e-krishi, practicing tele-medicine in rural areas, achieving financial inclusion, promoting green jobs, etc. Through these initiatives, the Foundation aims to build knowledge societies with the vision to reduce poverty by investing in the development of human capital, thereby building skills and making knowledge available to all members of civil society for long-term sustainable development.

The mission of the Foundation is to develop a path for people-focussed inclusive growth driven by knowledge, technology and innovation. The Foundation focusses on creating micro units of excellence and innovation through entrepreneurship for better productivity and competitiveness by accelerating Panchayat centric development with people's participation.

The Government of Kerala has been observing 19 June as the 'Day of Reading' for the past 21 years to commemorate the annual remembrance day of P.N. Panicker, father of Library and Literacy Movement of Kerala. Based on the overwhelming response to the day-long activities to inculcate reading habit and foster book-mindedness among school and college students and underprivileged sections of society, the government has now declared a Reading Month, initiating month-long celebration and activities in schools, colleges, panchayats, etc. Now, Reading Month celebrations are observed in all the 28 states and 9 union territories of India as well as 9 foreign countries. The message of reading and development initiated by the P.N. Panicker Foundation through this movement has reached 3.15 million population of the country.

The Foundation organized internet-enabled reading

in 2002 (digital reading). This paved the way for the establishment of 25,000 rural home e-libraries through internet connectivity. In its efforts to make Kerala the first state in the country to attain full digital literacy, the Foundation has made 5.25 lakh ordinary citizens digitally literate as per the norms of the Pradhan Mantri Gramin Digital Saksharta Abhiyan. As a second stage of this programme, the Foundation established 18 digital libraries across the state with the concept of repositioning the libraries as knowledge hubs to promote knowledge societies.

The Foundation has initiated Knowledge Economy and Green Economy programmes, establishing knowledge societies in over 2 lakh panchayats in a phased manner by establishing digital libraries. The prestigious programme, with a budget of 1,200 crore provided by the Government of India, was launched on 19 June 2018. The project was dedicated to the memory of P.N. Panicker at a function held at Vigyan Bhavan, New Delhi, and was attended by numerous ministers and secretaries from the Ministry of Human Resource Development and Ministry of Culture.

The P.N. Panicker Foundation has been honoured with the prestigious National Award for Outstanding Efforts in Science and Technology Communication (Category-A) for the year 2021. This recognition, instituted by the Ministry of Science and Technology, Government of India, acknowledges the Foundation's significant impact over the last five years in the field of science and technology communication. The award consisted of a cash prize of five lakh, a memento and a citation which was conferred during the award distribution function organized as part of National Science Day celebrations on 28 February 2022 at Vigyan Bhavan, New Delhi, by Dr Jitendra Singh, Hon'ble Minister of State for Science and Technology (Independent Charge), Prime Minister's Office and Departments of Atomic Energy and Space, Government of India.

www.ingramcontent.com/pod-product-compliance
Lightning Source LLC
LaVergne TN
LVHW090543110826
845146LV00003B/1245

* 9 7 8 9 3 5 7 0 2 3 9 9 3 *